A Woman's SEARCH *For Her* PURPOSE

A Woman's SEARCH *For Her* PURPOSE

A Woman's Journey to Emotional Enlightenment

Mona L. Martin

PALMETTO
P U B L I S H I N G
Charleston, SC
www.PalmettoPublishing.com

Copyright © 2024 by Mona L. Martin

All rights reserved

No portion of this book may be reproduced, stored in a retrieval system, or transmitted in any form by any means—electronic, mechanical, photocopy, recording, or other—except for brief quotations in printed reviews, without prior permission of the author.

Paperback ISBN: 9798822961661

Dedication

This is a brief story of the trials and tribulations in my life. I am telling this story through what I observed growing up. My perception changed dramatically as I grew and evolved over the years, but this is part of my healing journey through life.

I want to dedicate this book to my parents, my siblings, my ex-husband, and most of all my children and grandchildren. If it weren't for all of you, I would not be the woman that stands here strong and vibrant today. I have such gratitude and appreciation for what you all have taught me and continue to teach me daily. Through all the tumultuous times that we have been through, I have chosen wisdom over being wounded, love over hate, and joy over anger. Every time my father hit me, I gained strength; every time my mother wasn't there for me, I chose to be present, available, and loving to my children. Every time my husband pushed me away, I turned within myself, which is priceless. I thank you all, my children and grandchildren, for teaching me new perspectives and unconditional love every day. If it were not for all of you, I would not have learned to see the world through a different lens. And for this, I am eternally grateful.

I also want to thank my role models, who have helped me tremendously through my journey of self-discovery: Tony Robbins, Abraham Hicks, Christy Whitman, Sadh Guru, the late Dr. Wayne W. Dwyer, Kain Ramsey, and of course my good spiritual friend Jessica.

I pray that this book can enlighten someone in their life and that it gets into the hands of someone who needs to hear this message. I pray that people continue to work on their healing journeys, always put themselves first, love fully, and have compassion for everyone. Everyone has a story to tell, which is priceless and full of treasures if you choose to open your chest and learn the lessons.

I have learned that doing the inner work is a beautiful journey, and I have loved every minute of it. I have learned so much about myself, my strength, my tenacity, and my courage, and I am so proud of how much I have learned. I have turned into a strong, vibrant woman who knows her worth, and I have chosen to help other women know theirs. Always remember that life is always working for us, not against us.

Contents

Chapter 1:	*My Family*	*1*
Chapter 2:	*My First Two Husbands*	*17*
Chapter 3:	*My Mother*	*38*
Chapter 4:	*The Psychic*	*46*
Chapter 5:	*The Psychic and the Chakras?*	*62*
Chapter 6:	*Putting the Pieces Together*	*73*
Chapter 7:	*My Sister*	*85*
Chapter 8:	*New York*	*94*
Chapter 9:	*My Spiritual Awakening*	*109*
Chapter 10:	*My Healing Journey*	*121*
Chapter 11:	*Lessons Learned*	*128*
About the Author		*132*

1

My Family

Why do people behave the way they do? Why do I see the things that I see? These have always been provocative questions in my life since I was a little girl. Why does my father get so mad at the simplest things? What is making him so angry? When I say mad, I mean psychotic, angry mad! Why does my mom not care about me or my siblings, and why is she so emotionally and mentally detached from life, or should I say checked out?

Why did my parents have four kids—three biological and one adopted—and not give two shits about them? I could never understand why they had so many kids and chose not to be a part of their lives or teach them the valuable lessons that they so desperately needed to learn. I mean, they fed us, clothed us, and put a roof over our heads, but that was it. What values do you have when you have five kids running around, doing whatever they want, and the eldest, an eleven-year-old girl, is responsible for watching them all while you work? I know times were tough back then, and they could not afford a babysitter or daycare, but I felt empathy for my sister, and the responsibility that was laid on her was excruciating to watch. Can you imagine an eleven-year-old becoming a single parent to four kids? This was how I thought back then, and this was what I saw.

I remember being very afraid of my father, and if we acted up during the day, we knew we were going to get it when he got home from work. I had a twin brother, and we were always called the terrible twins! Why we were called that was beyond me, and we bore the brunt of his anger. "You're as dumb as Banum's bitch who jumped in the river to get out of the rain!" I heard my father say that repeatedly over my life. To this day I have no idea what he meant by that. As I said my father was an incredibly angry man; he yelled and screamed constantly. This behavior could have come from his military background as he was in the army, or it could have come from his upbringing. He would never talk to us kids; yelling and screaming was the norm in that house, but when he yelled and screamed, people ran to him and listened.

When he punished me, he would do so with anything that he could get his hands on at that moment. It could be with willow switches from the lilac tree in our backyard; he had me go out to the backyard and pick one that he was to use on me. I would always choose the thin ones, thinking that they would not hurt as much as the thick branches. But little did I know that was not the case. He would bend me over his knee and use a leather belt on me until I was black and blue. My mother used to stand there and watch, and after a while, she would tell him, "That's enough!" And my father would shove me off his lap. Other times he would grab paddles and use those on me—you know, the ones that had a rubber band and a ball attached to it. He used to rip the rubber band and the ball off and use the paddle.

I found out as I got older that my father was abusing not just me but my other siblings as well, and he violated my sister! Who are these people? Why did I choose to live in an environment like this? I thought that there were going to be some hard lessons that I was going to have to learn through these experiences. These were the questions my nine-year-old self was asking, and these are the experiences that I have observed and noticed so far in my life. You would think these experiences would last a person a lifetime. Oh, no, I have only just begun.

My father was an only child, and my mother only had one sister. Over the years I thought about how they were brought up as children themselves. I could not imagine that their lives growing up were a bed of roses; I could only assume through their actions and behaviors. I know that my father's father, my grandfather, was an extremely industrious worker;

he worked in granite quarries for a living, and he built his own house from the ground up. My grandmother worked in a safety pin company. I saw that they were both alcoholics. The minute they woke up in the morning, they would put a splash of Seagram's Crown Royal whiskey in their coffee. They started their day like that, and they drank all day. I observed this growing up, and I did not want to have any type of relationship with them. I saw how they acted when they were drinking, and it scared me as a young child. I could only imagine what that was like for my father growing up.

I am not sure if my grandfather was a happy drunk or a mean drunk. As a child, I did not see him being mean while he drank, but I'm not sure how he was to my father growing up. Back then I did not care as a child; all I knew was that he was drunk, period, and so was my grandmother. She was a short, petite woman, but when she drank, she became feisty. You have heard the old saying "Dynamite comes in small packages." That was her.

But I must think back and wonder what type of father my grandfather was to my father. For my father to be as angry and mad as he was every day, there had to be some deep-rooted issues there because the strongest role model for any child is the parent of the same sex. I have no idea what kind of nurturing my grandmother gave to my father. I could just assume that she did not give him any, and my grandfather was just as angry as he was. I am only looking from my perception as a child at that time and their behavior. I saw them drinking all the time. Did they do that growing up with my father? Did my father see them drink as much as I did? Were they angry drunks? I do not know; I am making assumptions while trying to put the pieces of this puzzle together. My father and my mother never really talked about their upbringing; they would only tell us bits and pieces.

And then there was my mother, coming from a household where there was her, her sister (my aunt), her mother (my grandmother), and their father (my grandfather). individuals labeled my grandmother with a mental illness; I saw at an incredibly early age that she was a pill popper and an alcoholic as well. I'm not sure why my grandmother had that label, but I found out later in life that my grandfather cheated on her with my grandmother's sister! Hmm, something to think about. The labels that were shot around back then blew my mind; to this day labels that are put on people get to me. Did anyone stop to think that my grandmother just wanted someone to be there for her, to listen to her, and to understand what she was going through when my grandfather cheated on her with her sister? Did anyone care how she was feeling during that situation, or did people just avoid her? My answer would be the latter. That would play a huge part in someone's psyche.

I saw that my grandmother did anything for attention, from falling on the ground all the time to shitting her pants in public. It was a cry for help and attention from anyone who would give it to her. Any attention, whether it be good or bad, was better than none at all.

My grandfather never told my mother or my aunt that he loved them. I remember my mother telling me that she asked her father why he never told them that he loved them, and he replied, "I never told you I didn't." I could only imagine how my mother and aunt internalized that. My grandfather would always wake up my mother and aunt when there was a thunderstorm outside and make them sit on the couch until it was over; why? I don't know what my mother told me. And I remember my grandfather's Kinesthetics; he was not the type of person that looked like he was open to any relationship or conversation. He always had a stern look on his face, and I did not feel comfortable going around him, or I never really wanted to have a conversation with him. He reminded me of Scrooge, the old miser; every time I looked at him, that was whom I thought of. He looked like that type of guy who was just mean and tight with his money. I remember him always sitting in the chair in the corner, reading a *National Geographic* magazine. I always had this uneasy feeling when I was around him; I was intimidated by him.

And as a child, I noticed that my grandmother did not have that close of a relationship with my mother and my aunt. I could see that she was emotionally and mentally not present. I remember going to her house every Sunday for dinner, and she would always cook fried chicken. I remember the whole family packing up in a car, two kids in the hatchback, three kids in the back seat, and my parents in the front seat. Back then we did not even worry about seat belts! Yes, those were the good old days. While she was cooking fried chicken, I would watch her pop pills and suck down the alcohol. When we would sit down for our meal, I would watch her; there was something wrong with the way she swallowed her food because every time she took a bite, she had to grab her throat and twist it to help the food go down her esophagus. That used to freak me out as a child, especially while I was eating. I was told by my mother later that she had swallowed some Drano pipe cleaner for the sink, and that was why she had to do that. This made me think, "Did she try to commit suicide at one point in her life? And why would she do that? Could that be the reason she was labeled mentally ill?" I just don't know.

Getting back to my mother, I could only assume that she did not have a well-rounded childhood either because of my grandmother's actions as a mother and her behavior. This is where generations start to repeat patterns. My mother was labeled with a mental illness, and she was considered disabled at the age of forty-two. I remember I was in the hospital with appendicitis when she came to visit me, and she told me that she qualified for disability. Why she was labeled disabled was beyond me. Back then she never really worked long at any job, and I just concluded that she did not want to work. And I think working for the state was a big advantage for her going on social security disability. My mother knew people in the system to help her; she had connections. She was a supervisor for the Office of Child Support. It was oxymoronic being a supervisor for them, making home visits to people's houses, and guiding them on how to take care of their children when she could not even take care of her own children! Mind-blowing, huh? It makes you ask the question "How many people in this world have jobs they are truly not qualified for?" I saw back then that she did not have the experience or a degree to be in that position. Just saying. Anyhow my mother had told us that she had encephalitis of the brain stem, which was an inflammatory disease affecting the midbrain, pons, and medulla oblongata. That was her disability, which did not make sense to me because she had a clever mind, and she moved around quite well, especially if you gave her a cart in Costco!

My mother also had nine lives. She had had so many accidents in her life: falling down a whole flight of stairs at my brother's house and breaking multiple ribs and arms, falling several times at my sister's house and getting injured, and being in many car accidents. She had a perfect likeness to her mother; growing up and observing these accidents happening to my grandmother and mother and seeing the similarities between both, I wasn't sure if they truly were accidents or if they both were doing it for attention.

My mother was always emotionally and mentally detached from her feelings and her kids, just like her own mother. She was never there when I needed her; I learned at an incredibly early age that I could not depend or count on her for anything. I would try to have conversations with her, but she was never present at any given moment. I remember when I started my period at the age of twelve, she threw me a sanitary pad and a garter belt and said, "Here, put this on." She never had a conversation with me about my menstrual cycle or the changes of becoming a woman—nothing. I learned that she could not give me what I needed as a young girl or when I grew to be a woman. I learned that I had to do things on my own without any help from her.

I would watch my sister fight and argue with her and get so pissed off at her about everything; those two, in my eyes, had the most toxic relationship that I have ever observed in my life! I could see that my sister was fighting so hard to have any type of relationship with her with no resolution. Watching those two, I decided that my mother was not worth fighting over. I did not want that dynamic in any relationship. Why fight with anyone who is not emotionally or mentally there? It is like fighting with an alcoholic; you are never going to get anywhere. That was what I saw. I learned at an incredibly early age that my mother and my father were my biggest teachers in life; they are whom I do not want to be when I grow up! This family whom I am living with right now is definitely not the one that I will have when I grow up. This is where I must learn what *discernment* truly means.

The things that I observed and heard growing up with my mother would blow anyone's mind. I remember when her aunt was in the hospital with pancreatic cancer, dying, her sister and she were raiding their aunt's house, taking and selling all her stuff. My sister was there during the process, and I could not understand why she was so mad at my aunt and not my mother. I remember having conversations with my sister over this whole situation, and she would tell me that she was yelling and screaming at my aunt because she was taking stuff out of their aunt's house. I was thinking, "So is Mom! Why are you not angry with Mom as well? This is just batshit crazy! Why would you hold one person accountable for their actions and not the other? They are both doing the same thing." This was how I perceived this specific situation. I could not understand the logic.

Another time, my sister and I went up to my parents' house to visit them, I did not know at the time that my sister was going to confront my father about him violating her. I remember that day clearly because of what my mother said; it sticks in my head till this day. My mother sat there on the couch after she confronted my father and said, "Well, there is nothing I can do about it now, and I would not have done anything back then because I could not have been able to raise five kids by myself!"

"What the hell did I just hear!" I would think about my sister, "Why would you want a relationship with her when she just said that to you? Is it just me who notices this shit and what she just said? Who says this? What mother would stay with any man who she just found out had violated her daughter?" That comment made me feel that my mother had total disregard for the experience that my sister went through when it happened, and she showed no sympathy whatsoever toward my sister. At that moment I saw that my mother was only thinking of herself and not the victim, period.

The hurt that I felt for my sister was immeasurable. "This is fucked up! This is the family that I have been growing up with all my life." You start to question life when you are living with people like this, and you start asking the bigger questions in life. "Why am I here, and what is my purpose for being here? Why should any kid have to observe any of this insanity growing up?"

My mother and my father did not have a clue about how to be parents, and they really should not have even been married because they fought all the time. My mother was always sneaky with everything that she did; she would sneak food, buy things, and hide them, and my father was always pissed at everything that my mother did. I did watch my father try to be affectionate with my mother; several times he would try and give her hugs and a kiss, but she would brush him off like he did not exist. And my mother was just not there at all mentally or emotionally; maybe my father felt like he wasn't loved when he was a kid, and he wasn't getting love from my mother, so he was so frustrated and mad and was doing anything that he knew how to get any attention.

And my mother was emotionally and mentally disconnected; she didn't know how to love because she had never observed it with her parents, and my mother saw that my grandmother was emotionally and mentally disconnected from her husband and her kids. These are the patterns of life that we need to seriously look at, my friend. I learned so many lessons growing up in that environment: who I do not want to be as a parent, how to love and protect my children and be present and available for them (when I do have kids), and to tell them that I love them every single day. I had to learn everything that I knew on my own. I was learning noticeably young that these are the patterns and karmic cycles that must be broken. I can't allow these cycles to continue in future generations.

I was born on February 5, 1964. My mother always said that I was born on the day the Beatles came to America. But they arrived on February 7, 1964. I had a twin; my brother was born seven minutes after me. My mother did not have any idea she was having twins until the day she was in labor;

after I was born, she said she felt like she had to push again, and there was my twin brother. This made me think that the only way my mother would not have known if she was carrying twins was if she did not go to any prenatal checkups or doctor's appointments or if she did not have an ultrasound done. I know the ultrasound was invented in 1956 by Engr. Tom Brown and OB Ian Donald. So I know she could have had an ultrasound because it was invented at the time of our birth. Emotionally and mentally checked out!

Anyhow, when I was born, my mother did not have a name picked out for me because she was expecting to give birth to a boy this time and had a name picked out for him, but she did not have one picked out for a girl. I was born first before my twin brother, so the nurse who was in the labor and delivery room that day suggested calling me Mona. That was how my life started: I was not expected to be born, and I definitely did not have a name.

After my twin brother and I were born, my mother and father had one more child, my younger brother, and they adopted my cousin because my mother's sister did not want him and was going to put him in a foster home. My aunt was a partyer and did not want to be burdened with a child. I remember she lived with us for a little while, and she would go out to the bars at night and bring home some of the band members; they would be camped out on the living room floor in the morning. And I remember my father used to get pissed.

So I guess you could consider her a groupie back then. Even though my cousin was adopted, I always considered him my brother; we were close growing up. I babysat him a lot when my aunt was not there and my parents were working. My cousin, or should I say my brother, was born on my and my twin brother's seventh birthday!

There was a total of five kids in the house. Growing up in this house was not easy. Both my mother and father worked, and my sister, at the age of eleven, was responsible for us when they were at work. It was hell in that house; we did what we wanted to do with no supervision whatsoever. My sister did what she could but none of us wanted to listen to her or do what she wanted us to do, which would piss my parents off. My parents were called repeatedly at work to let them know what was going on at home. When my father got home, he would hit us with anything that would get his hand first. Again it was mostly the twins who got the brunt of his anger. As I grew older, I was told that my father beat my younger brother as well, hitting him so badly to the point that he couldn't breathe. My escape from all this turmoil that was going on at home was to go to the roller-skating rink every weekend.

I do not ever remember my sister getting hit because I was told she was the firstborn, and she was their favorite. That was embedded into my head at an early age when I heard it mentioned repeatedly by my parents and grandparents. It was like my sister could not do any wrong or get into trouble for anything. (At least that was what I thought, not knowing at that time what my father had done to her.) I would ask myself, "Why is she not ever getting punished for anything, while everyone else is?" I never saw my adopted brother ever get punished or beaten.

So my father never hit my sister and adopted brother. But he did violate my sister at the age of thirteen. My sister told me this, and I asked her why she did not say anything to anybody. She said that she did not want to feel like she was the reason why the family broke up. I could understand where she was coming from; as a victim of abuse, I'm sure she was going through feelings of shame and guilt and thinking it was her fault. These are just a few of what victims feel inside themselves. And I was thinking, "God, I hated doing this because I was judging her, but why would you want this dysfunctional family to stay together? Why would you not want it broken up? This household is not healthy! I would rather come from a broken home than the one I am in now! This is just sick!" She could see daily that her brothers and I were being beaten, and she didn't want to say or do anything?

I cannot even fathom what is going through a person's mind to abuse their children. I cannot wrap that shit around my head. Did my father beat on me and both of my brothers all the time because of what he did to my sister? Was he frustrated because he was not getting any love from my mother or he never got love from his parents? Was he so angry and frustrated that he had to take it out on someone? And I also thought, "Did he never beat on my sister because he violated her?" He felt guilty and ashamed of what he had done to her. I was seeing that this was child abuse, and I was also feeling I would probably never have the answers to these questions. Remember, I was ten years old when all this was happening! Why would any ten-year-old be asking all these questions about life at this age? This was the way I was perceiving things at the age of ten.

The day I turned eighteen, I faced my father and his abuse; we were nose to nose when I told him if he ever laid another hand on me again, I would drop him to the floor quicker than shit, and he would not know what hit him. I was scared shitless! I thought he was going to either stop or hit me again; it was a chance that I had to take. From that day forward, my father never laid another hand on me again. And our relationship took off on a different trajectory. That was the day that I learned to stand in my power! And I moved out of the house and met my first husband.

2

My First Two Husbands

I met my first husband at a cleaning company where I worked. He was my first love; I loved the person he was, his character, his personality, and his perseverance. He was very family-oriented. He was the very first boyfriend I had ever had. I had never dated before, so this was foreign to me.

When I first met him, he was just breaking up with a woman whom he had been in a relationship with for a while, and he was heartbroken over her because he loved her and her kids. I remember our first date with each other. I remember begging my father to borrow his car so we could go out. My father had just bought a brand-new Plymouth Horizon, he was very trepidatious about me taking it, and it took me a lot of coaxing before he let me borrow it. And so my new boyfriend and I went to a bar that night, and we both got so drunk. The whole date was about how heartbroken he was about breaking up with his ex, so we just drank all night to numb his pain.

When we were driving home, with me behind the wheel, it was two in the morning. I went to put a cigarette out in the ashtray, I swerved toward a tree, and I hit it. Neither one of us had our seat belts on, and the car went end over end. I remember it felt like I was in a tornado, spinning around and around, and I could hear glass shattering, and it was like in slow motion. Then I was shot out of the car, as well as my boyfriend.

When I woke up, I was in the middle of the road, lying flat on my back. I got up from the middle of the road, and I looked over to my right, and the car and my boyfriend were over an embankment. I stumbled over to the embankment and plopped down in the snowbank; that was when I saw the car. It was crushed like an accordion, with the radio still playing. My boyfriend was face down in the snowbank; he had a silk vest on. I remember looking at him as he lay there in the snowbank, and the back of his vest was all wet; I thought it was blood. I thought I killed him; at that point we had only been dating for two weeks.

He got up, and we both noticed that we did not have any broken bones, but I did need some stitches on my face because I had two lacerations, one under my right eye and one on the right side of my chin. As we were walking down the road so we could call an ambulance, he looked at me, saw the remains of the accident, and said, "*You done good, babe!* We are alive!" I found it amusing that he was trying to clean all the broken glass from the road as we were walking.

We ended up at a motel that was a little way down the road, and a couple let us in so we could call an ambulance. We both went to the hospital, and my father came there at four in the morning. He said that he went and looked at the car before he went to the hospital. When he got there, I thought he was going to be so mad at me because he had only had his car, which I just totaled, for two weeks. But the only thing that he said to me was, "Don't worry about it, it needed a new oil change anyways!" And he cried; he was so grateful that I was alive! That was when my relationship with my father started to take a turn for the better.

And that was the beginning of my and my boyfriend's relationship. It was difficult; we were both working and trying, like everyone else, to keep our heads above water, living paycheck to paycheck. I did not know how to be in a relationship; I did not know how to love because I was never taught it as a younger child. I was emotionally unstable. I did not know how to let someone love me because it was foreign to me. It scared me. He tried so hard to love me.

After being together for three years, we decided to get married. Four months after we got married, we joined a health club. They had a drawing for an all-expense-paid trip to the Bahamas, and I won! I considered this our honeymoon—until my sister decided that she wanted to go with us. At the time, I did not want her to go; I just wanted to be alone with my new husband. She begged and pleaded, and she and her husband ended up coming with us on our vacation. It was the very first time I had ever flown in an airplane, and it was the very first trip that I had ever taken in my life.

We had a beautiful time in the Bahamas. I will never forget that trip. My husband wasted a whole roll of film on lizards.

My sister was always a heavyset girl, and she was very self-conscious of herself and having her picture taken. I remember her telling me that she had a dream one night in the Bahamas that she sprained her ankle, and she woke up the next morning limping on that ankle; she was hobbling all day. We went to the beach that day, and she and her husband were walking down the beach hand in hand. My husband and I were walking behind them, and my husband took a picture of them. (I have that picture in my photo album.) My sister was so mad at my husband for taking that picture of her in a bathing suit! She said to him, "I don't want anyone seeing me limping down the beach!"

My husband said, "How are they going to tell you are limping in the picture?" LOL.

Anyhow, when we returned from the trip, I then became pregnant with my first child. I got pregnant in the Bahamas! I was twenty-three years old. I had a full-term pregnancy, and it went well; I did not have any issues. I remember going into labor late at night, and I wanted to stay home because I did not want to be in labor at that moment. I remember saying, "Can we do this tomorrow?" I ended up going to the hospital. I was in labor for 36½ hours (about one and a half days) and tried pushing for a couple of hours. I found out that my cervix was too narrow, and I had to have a C-section.

On January 15, 1987, my first son was born. My husband and I named him Billy. I did not get to see Billy after he was born because when they were doing their check up on him, they noticed that the blood was not flowing from his heart to his lungs, and they saw him turning blue, so they rushed him on a medevac flight to Boston Children's Hospital when he was twelve hours old. I was devastated and scared; I did not know what was going on. The hospital in Boston told us that they had to do surgery on him to put a shunt in so the blood could flow freely. Billy had open-heart surgery when he was twelve hours old. Everything happened so fast that I did not have time to process everything. "I am stuck in a hospital, healing from a C-section in Vermont, while Billy was whisked away before I got to see him in Boston for open-heart surgery! Why am I going through this? Why should anyone have to go through this?" It was hell! I was so distraught and so numb; I definitely was going through separation anxiety and postpartum depression. My husband was incredibly supportive and was there every step of the way.

Boston Children's Hospital stayed connected with us

constantly to let us know of Billy's condition; they also sent us all kinds of pictures of him, for which we were both so grateful! Billy's surgery went fine, and after three days, they flew him back to the hospital where I was still recovering from a C-section, and we were able to be with him. My heart was full. That was the first time in my whole life that I was truly engrossed with what love was; it was euphoric when I was able to hold my son for the first time. I did not know what love was growing up in the household that I grew up in because it was not shown to me; I did not know what love was when my husband was trying to show it to me. But the minute I held on to something that my husband and I created, it hit me! I felt like this child had a traumatic experience coming into this world, and I had to do everything that I could to protect him.

I spent a lot of time with Billy when he got out of the hospital. I gave him more attention than I did my husband. Billy was eight months old when my husband told me that he had an affair. I was devastated. After everything that we had been through, he told me this! He told me that he wanted to work things out, but I told him no because back then I felt like once someone cheats on you, there is no trust left, and there is nothing to work out. I did not want to give him a second chance. I was so mad at him and heartbroken; when he told me, Billy was in his crib, I hit the wall, and the shelf fell into Billy's crib; it missed him, thank God, but I was pissed and angry and frustrated!

So I moved out and back in with my parents. I did not want to do that, but I had no other choice. I did not stay there for long because I moved in with a couple of my friends. It took me eight months to get on my feet and find a place to live that was suitable for Billy and me. I had also filed for divorce, and I had a court date set for May 25, 1988. During this time my husband was with his new girlfriend, the woman whom he cheated on me with; he had moved in and started a new life with her. She had two kids from a previous marriage, and she could not have any more kids because she had her tubes tied. This was what my husband told me because at that time I thought he was going to get her pregnant, and even though we were getting a divorce, I still loved him very much.

I was in the process of moving into our new apartment when tragedy struck. I was working, and it was like any other normal day. I dropped Billy off at daycare before I went to work. A police officer came into my workplace, and I saw him talking to my boss; I did not know what it was for. But my boss came up to me and told me that the police officer wanted to talk to me. I was scared; I did not do anything, and I did not know what was going on. He told me to follow him, and so I did. He told me to get into the police car, and

I did. And I kept asking him what was going on, and he started to take me to the day care provider's house, which was just down the road from where I worked.

While he was driving, an ambulance with sirens pulled out in front of us, and we were following them. That was when the police officer said that something has happened to Billy. I did not know what was going on; my life just stopped and stood still at that moment. Time collapsed. Everything at that moment was in slow motion—the police officers, the EMTs from the ambulance, every person, every movement.

When I got to her home, the day care provider was hysterical! She was screaming and apologizing to me at the top of her lungs. She then proceeded to tell me that she had laid Billy down for a nap and went to check on him after a while, and he was not breathing. She then called the ambulance and the police. The ambulance took Billy to the hospital, and I followed them with the police officer.

When I got to the hospital, the doctors and nurses let me know that Billy had passed away. I was emotionally hysterical and numb! I called my soon-to-be ex-husband to let him know what happened, and he and his girlfriend showed up at the hospital. At the time, I did not think that was the time or place for her to be there; I just wanted my husband. I was hysterical, I was devastated, and his girlfriend commented, "I know what you're going through, and I'm sorry!"

I remember screaming at her at the top of my lungs in front of him in the middle of the hospital, "You have no idea what I am going through because you have two beautiful, healthy boys who are still fuckin' alive, and you stole my husband, whom I still love very much! You do not belong here!" A priest and some doctors and nurses then brought me into a room in the hospital to calm me down, and once I was as calm as I could be, they brought me into the room where Billy was in. He was lying on the gurney, wrapped up in a blanket. The doctor asked me if I wanted to hold him one more time, but I felt like I could not go near him; it traumatized me to see that! That is a memory that is forever etched in my brain. He was lying down on that gurney, wrapped up like a burrito. Billy had passed away in his sleep. A blood clot formed over his shunt and stopped the blood flowing from his heart to his lungs, and it killed him. He was sixteen months old when he passed.

This was May 24, 1988. Exactly twenty-four hours later, on May 25, 1988, I was in a courtroom, getting a divorce from my husband. I was only twenty-four years old. Again I had to move back in with my parents; I was so distraught! I had lost my whole life in twenty-four hours, and I did not know how I was going to surpass this. I was numb for one month. I stayed in my bedroom at my parents' house and did not want to talk to or be around anyone. I just sat there

Indian-style on the bed, rocked back and forth, and cried and cried and cried. I remember my dad coming into my room and hugging me, and he broke down crying, which was the first time I ever saw him cry. He would not let go of me; that was the first time I had felt compassionate love from my father, which made me cry even harder because I needed that from him.

One month after Billy passed away and I was divorced, my friends got me out of the house to go out and just change my environment. We went to a bar, and that was when I met my soon-to-be second husband. He was an extremely outgoing guy. He had a lot of friends and knew a lot of people, and I mean a lot! I learned a lot from him; he taught me from the beginning of our relationship to not care about what other people thought of me and to be who I wanted to be, and if people do not like it, too bad. We started dating right off; plus, I did not want to continue to stay at my parents' house, so we immediately moved in with each other.

It did not take me long at all to realize that he was a full-blown drug abuser and alcoholic. No wonder he was an outgoing guy and knew a lot of people. Now I knew. With every paycheck that he would get, he would be in the bars, blowing it on drugs and alcohol, while I was paying all the bills out of my paycheck. I remember he got paid on a Friday and blew his whole paycheck by Saturday and tried going into my pocketbook to steal my money so he could do more drugs and drink more. He was 6′2″, weighing about 210 lb., and I remember I pinned him on the bed because he was trying to steal money out of my pocketbook. I wasn't allowing it.

I came to realize through our relationship that he was married before me, and he used to beat on his first wife, who ended up in the hospital. He never laid a single hand on me. He knew that I was a tough bitch, and I was not going to take anyone's shit. (Thanks, Dad, for beating on me growing up and teaching me strength. It was what he had taught me, right?) I was not going to let this boyfriend walk all over me. He was in and out of bars and cheating with every woman imaginable. His whole family were full-blown alcoholics and drug abusers. From cocaine to acid to heroin to mushrooms, you name it, they did it. I observed so much from this family and watched all the drugs and alcohol that they either ingested, consumed, or shot up.

I used to smoke marijuana with his father. That was the hardest drug I ever did because I was watching how everyone else was acting on the other drugs, and I did not want any part of them. Smoking pot relaxed me, it took away the anxiety, and I did not think as much.

I remember a time we were both staying with a woman whom he was friends with (I'm sure now he slept with her back then). She was a big-time cocaine dealer, and she had just bought an eight ball of cocaine. She had it on her kitchen table, cutting it up to distribute and sell. She had a customer come over to buy some who was eight months pregnant! I watched her put a rubber band around her arm and inject cocaine into her arm at eight months pregnant! I could not believe what I was seeing, and while she was doing that, the police were knocking on her door because her daughter had just gotten caught at the local drugstore stealing all kinds of stuff. When she saw that a police officer was at her door, she took that whole eight ball and swiped it off her kitchen table and onto the floor, and the pregnant woman ran into the bathroom. I am not shitting you; it was a true story! I was thinking I was going to get arrested for that eight ball on the ground only for being guilty by association and being in the wrong place at the wrong time. The police officer never came into the house and just brought her daughter home. That was too close to home for me; we moved out of there after that incident.

I started to see synchronicities. At the time, his brother Todd was dating my ex-husband's ex-girlfriend—you know, the one whom my ex loved along with her two kids—and we were getting drunk over it on our first date and got into a car accident. Coincidence? I think not. And they got married! After a while, Todd's drug abuse got to him, and he passed away, and so did his brother Timmy. I am telling you, these guys were hard core! Why I was watching this and putting up with this for three years was beyond me. I felt like I wanted to give my boyfriend a second chance and see if he would change because I never gave my ex-husband a second chance, and I wanted to see if I could help him get sober.

Next thing you know, I found out that I was pregnant again, this time with twins! I was so ecstatic. So my boyfriend and I decided to get married; we thought that was the right thing to do. Do not ask me why. I was twenty-six years old at this point in my life.

Being pregnant while with a full-blown alcoholic and drug abuser took a huge toll on my well-being and the welfare of my children. Again, my second husband was in the bars every time he got paid, and he was cheating on me with so many women that I could not manage it anymore; he was not changing even though he promised he would. One time when I was five months pregnant, I pushed him down a flight of stairs because I hated what he was doing to me and my family. He came charging up those stairs after me, and I was afraid for me and my kids. I did not have a clue about what he was going to do to us. He realized how mad he was, and he stopped. I never knew, with the number of women he had slept around with, if he was going to come home with a venereal disease. The stress of this relationship finally took its toll on me, and I went into premature labor at twenty-six weeks (about six months).

While I was going into premature labor, my mother's father passed away. Between my second husband's escapades and my grandfather, this was just too much to manage. I went to the hospital, and they told me that I had to stay there for the duration of my pregnancy, for the next three months. I was willing to do anything to save my kids. So there I stayed. But after a week, they could not stop the labor, and I had to have an emergency C-section to try to save the kids, but they gave them a 5 percent chance of living.

On May 26, 1990, I gave birth to two boys. My first son weighed in at 1 lb. 11 oz., and Justin weighed in at 1 lb. 5 oz. I remember when they pulled Justin out of my stomach, his cry sounded like a Siamese cat. They had asked me if I wanted to see them, and I told them no because I thought if they did not survive and I saw them, I would become attached to them. Also, I had the memory of Billy lying there on that gurney in the hospital etched in my brain, and I was thinking of that. I did not see them until the next day. I went to the intensive care unit, and they were so tiny; they were the same size as my hand. They did not have any cartilage in their ears; they did not have slits in their eyes or their butts. I had never seen anything so small in my life. They had to tape their ears back so they would form. They also had Saran Wrap around their bodies to keep the heat in.

On May 28, 1990, two days after the twins were born, I was outside at the hospital, getting some fresh air, when the doctor came outside and told my husband and me that they needed to speak to us. We went back upstairs, and the doctor told us that Justin had just passed away because he was so premature, and his lungs were just too underdeveloped.

Why was this happening to me again? What did I do to deserve this? Why should anyone have to go through this? I blamed myself, I blamed my husband, I blamed God! My whole life I keep asking the question *why*, and I am not getting the answers that I needed to hear. I was just waiting to hear that my other son was going to die too. I could not take it. I was only twenty-six years old; I was in my second marriage, which was in complete shambles, and I had lost two kids! And while this was happening, my husband had lost yet another job and was still cheating on me. *I was done.* That was it. I kicked him to the curb and moved on with my life.

My son was my miracle baby. That boy fought so hard to stay alive and did! He was in the hospital for six months. I worked the night shift while he was in there, and then I went to the hospital every morning when I got out of work. I did not miss one day of visiting with him. My husband was never there. I remember every day when I went into that intensive care unit, I would ask the doctors and nurses, "How many grams did he gain today?" They used to draw all kinds of Disney baby characters and put them in his incubator because I told them that his nursery at home had Disney babies. And when I took him home, he was 6 lb. 6 oz., the size of a newborn.

That boy was stuck to my side like glue; I protected him so much. He came home with an oxygen saturation monitor, and I had to have a visiting nurse come to my house to check on him. It was arduous work, but he was my life; he fought to be with me, and I had to fight to be with him.

This boy had to be admitted to the hospital off and on because he was born so prematurely. He would come down with asthma and bronchitis because his lungs were so premature. I remember the board of directors and hospital staff came to my apartment one day and sat down and told me that the hospital bill for my son was over $1 million, and they wanted me to know that I did not have to worry about it because he was the smallest baby born at that hospital, and it was a miracle that he was alive. Plus, I was a single parent at that point. I was so grateful and so appreciative of the whole hospital staff and the amazing job that they did to keep my son alive. Words cannot express the gratitude I have for the staff at that hospital. This was when I started to believe in miracles because, to be honest, this was nothing but a miracle.

After I separated from and divorced my second husband, I needed to focus on myself and my son. I spent the next four years on my own with him. I decided to work on myself and start doing some inner reflection on my life. I was curious to learn why people act the way they do and why I have made so many piss-poor decisions in my life. My son's father was never a part of his life, and he never paid child support for him.

My child was growing up, and I was loving every minute of it. He was such a mama's boy; wherever I was, he was. He had to be always near me; he even slept with me in my bed. I tried putting him in his room several times, but I would wake up in the morning with him on the floor next to my bed with his pillow and blanket, which I did not have a problem with. I dated a couple of guys off and on, but they were nothing serious.

What I had learned at this time of my life was I cannot trust men; they are all cheaters. I could not turn to my mother for any support with all the issues I had gone through with men or the losses of my children, and I realized that I had made some stupid choices when it came to relationships. My father was trying to be supportive and help me when I was going through some tough times; at least he listened to me, and he started to tell me that he loved me, so I started to see my father trying to come around and be some sort of parent the best way he knew how.

I had never had a close relationship with my sister because she was so busy living her life. She had gone through a divorce as well and was trying to make ends meet by herself, and she suggested that I move in with her; she had bought a single-wide trailer and was living there, so we decided to split expenses. I lived with her for about a year with my son after

I divorced my second husband. My sister and I both worked for the same company, and she helped me get a job there.

I realized in that year of living with her that you had to always do things her way, and there was no other way to do things. Everything was meticulous and structured. At that time I noticed she only did things that she gained benefit from for her well-being. For years I thought that was a selfish behavior, only thinking of yourself and not others, but as I grew older, I realized that is such a beautiful quality to have. That woman knew her worth! It has absolutely nothing to do with selfishness; it's about knowing one's self-worth. And she wasn't wasting her precious time on minuscule shit.

But I did not know my worth at that time, so for me it was tough living with her. I felt like it was living with a mother I never had. Do you know what I am saying? I did not know how to manage that either because I never had a mother who would suggest to me what to do; that was foreign to me. My whole life I rebelled against people telling me what to do because it never felt right for me. I felt that with my parents and with my sister or anybody for that matter. I learned quickly from people that people don't like it when you don't do what they want you to do. I started to think, "Is it really my problem that they don't like it?" I started learning that what is good for one is not necessarily good for another.

So after about a year of living with my sister, she met a guy and moved in with him, and she was going to sell the trailer that we were living in. I had to find another place to live. While my sister was doing all this, I met my third husband at work. I started seeing more patterns. I thought, "Why are certain men entering my life when I have gone through so much shit and trauma? I'm becoming aware of a lot of things now."

When I first met him, I did not like him. He was the type of guy you did not want to take home to Mom or Dad for them to meet. But now that I think about it, why would I care what my parents thought when I never did before, right? Anyhow, he had long hair, he wore Harley-Davidson T-shirts, and he had tattoos on his arms. I was judging him by how he looked and not by who he was. Never judge a book by its cover. I played so hard to get with him. I just was not interested in him. He changed his whole appearance to get my attention: he cut his hair, he wore nice shirts, and he was such a pleasant guy to talk to. He was interested in who I was; I had never met anyone like that before in my life.

We started dating each other. He told me after we started dating that he remembered the first time he saw me walk down the hall at work with my sister, and he said to his friend, "I am going to marry that girl!" LOL. We found out we had a couple of things in common: we both were divorced, and he had a daughter from a previous marriage who was the same age as my son. They are three weeks apart. When we started dating, because my sister had sold her trailer, I moved back in with my parents again for a couple of months until my boyfriend and I could find a place of our own.

During our courtship he would call me three to four times a day, buy me flowers all the time, and buy me cards; he smothered me. That scared me because I was not used to it. I did not know how to manage it. I felt smothered, like, "Back off, please. This is too much!" Little did I know at that time that he was love-bombing me. I had relationships with guys who were both cheaters drug abusers and alcoholics. I did not know how to manage a guy who treated me nicely. It was like going from one end of the stick to the other.

Little did I know back then that he was teaching me my self-worth. I seriously did not know what love was with a partner. I had the love of my son, but having a partner to love was difficult for me. I came with a lot of baggage when he met me. I was broken from two marriages, and I had lost two kids. I was thirty-one. I definitely had all my defenses up and was not allowing anyone to break down my walls. I was unstable, and I was tough. I knew I did not want any bullshit from anyone. I was in my masculine energy, and I had become a very independent woman, not depending on anyone for support or help. It took a lot of adjusting for me.

When he entered the picture, I made it clear to him, saying, "If you could not accept my son"—who was four at the time—"you cannot have me. We are a joint package. And if you hurt my son, I will kick your ass to the curb quicker than crap!" I made the rules, and I made them clear before I even got involved with him. I had to be specific. My son's father had never been a part of his life after I divorced him, and I wanted a strong role model for him, and I truly felt this guy would be the one. Over time with this boy, I soon realized that he was a full-blown narcissist.

3

My Mother

The first five years of my life together with my new boyfriend were good, or so I thought. He and I never argued or fought, and we always had a good relationship. We had the most amazing sex life, and it was the best I have ever had or experienced. Then I became pregnant again; I was thirty-five years old at this point in my life. My son was eight. We were living in our apartment.

When I was six months pregnant, my father passed away from a massive coronary heart attack while at home at the age of fifty-nine, and my mother sat on the couch and did nothing about it. She did not call 911; she called 411 instead, and she did not even attempt to do CPR on him straight from her mouth. She said that she could not do CPR or even try to save him because he was so big. We had come to find out later that she had been having an affair with another guy for years; that was why she did not try to save him. After about two hours, my younger brother showed up at the house and was desperately doing CPR to save him and was unsuccessful. I could not imagine any child having to try to save their own father's life, while their mother sat on the couch and did absolutely nothing! Who does this? The guilt that that woman had to live with would be insurmountable.

After my father passed away, my boyfriend and I moved in with my mother. OMG, it was so against our will, but we did it because we felt like she could not live alone; plus, I got the impression that no one else wanted to take on the responsibility of doing it. And we had my son, I was pregnant with another, and we were in the process of getting custody of my boyfriend's daughter from a previous marriage, so we thought it would be cheaper to live there and split the expenses.

After we moved in, she cleaned out that trailer that they were living in and got rid of all of my father's stuff with no emotional attachment to anything. I never once saw her cry! I thought that was very odd. She was with my father for thirty-five years and had no emotions whatsoever. She functioned as if he never existed. Very robotic. This woman had no attachment to any of his things; she was trashing them left and right! I could not believe it. After she cleaned out the single-wide trailer, she wanted to trade it in for a double-wide trailer. Was she just erasing everything and all the memories that she had with my father? I did not get it.

While she was doing this, I went to the hospital and gave birth to another son. He was full-term and my healthiest baby. During my whole pregnancy, I was considered an elevated risk because of my age and my history of previous births, and I had to have my cervix sewn shut so I could carry him, which was very painful toward the end of the pregnancy. Without delay, I decided to get my tubes cut and tied because I was so grateful that I had two boys, and they were healthy. Plus, I was thinking about it. I was six months pregnant with my first pregnancy when my mother's father passed away, and I was six months pregnant with my third pregnancy when my father passed away. I did not know how to take that. I took time off from work to spend it with both of my sons and moved in with my mother.

So my boyfriend and I got married; this was my third marriage. During this time we were in the process of getting custody of my new husband's daughter because her mother chose to be with a man who violated a younger girl. My husband's daughter was only eight years old. I was starting to think, "How can I be living this life? I have been married three times, I have two boys, and I have had two sons who have passed away. We are getting custody of a girl whose mother chose a violator over her. I am living with my mother, who did the same thing that this woman is doing, choosing to stay with a man who has violated one of their children! And my mother has never been there for me and let my father die. What the hell was I thinking? This must have been insanity at its finest!"

After six months I went back to work. My husband and I decided it would be best if we worked on opposite night teams because there was no way in hell we were going to let my mother take care of our kids. It just was not an option for us. We always wanted either one of us home with the kids. We did this for five years; it was so hard that it started to take a toll on our marriage. My mother would do everything in her power to keep us up without sleep on the nights that we worked, and she would scream at our kids; she was just a miserable bitch! We would fight with her all the time. And with all this happening, my husband and I were drifting apart. We never saw each other; we would use up all our vacation time to spend with each other. And after a while, we both ended up having affairs with other people.

I met a guy at work, and I had an affair with him for one year. My husband and I were not spending much time with each other because of being on opposite shifts. Things did not last with this guy; he was married, and he did not want to get a divorce from his wife, whom he had been with for over twenty years. After a year the guilt was getting the best of me, and I ended up telling my husband about our affair.

I did not know at that time that my husband had an affair as well. He kept it hidden from me. The way I did find out was when he was sleeping because he had worked the night before. A sheriff came knocking at the door, and he gave me subpoena papers. I thought they had to do with us getting custody of his daughter. I opened the envelope and was shocked at what I was reading. The paperwork was asking my husband to pay child support for a kid he had had with a woman whom he had a one-night stand with!

"Are you fuckin' serious? This is a fuckin' nightmare! My whole life is just a soap opera. Why is all this following me and happening in my life? Do I have 'stupid, dumb bitch' written all over my forehead? This must be a fuckin' joke."

I was so pissed at him. I wanted to beat the shit out of him. And it was not because of what most people would think it would be. I was so pissed at him not for the fact that he had cheated on me but because I thought, "Who am I to be mad at something that he did when I did the same thing? That would be hypocritical." The reason I was pissed at him was that when the guilt was getting the best of me because I cheated on him, I came out and told him; that would have been the perfect time for him to tell me that he had a one-night stand, but he did not say a word. That was what made me so angry. So this woman had been pregnant for nine months and already had the baby, and he did not say a word to me. I struggled to be with someone who could not communicate with me.

My life at this point had been a shit show, and I must stop and do a lot more self-reflection. I needed to figure out why my life was going this way and what I was doing. I needed time to myself with my boys; I just wanted to focus on being the best mother that I could be to both of my sons. I was sick and tired of the game men were playing now. I did not want to trust any man, and I did not want to be with any man. I knew that I had always been cheated on, and this was the first time that I cheated on someone, and I did not like myself because of it. I felt like I needed to do a lot of soul-searching. I was just at the point in my life where I did not love myself, and if I did not love myself, how was I going to love somebody else?

I also could not stand living with my mother anymore; it was just too much dealing with her and what I had gone through with my husband. It was Thanksgiving Day 2003, and after six years of living with my mother, we moved out. I decided that my husband and I needed to separate for a while, but unfortunately, we could not afford a place with three kids, whom we were both responsible for, so we decided to rent a house and split the expenses. It was just too much for me to manage at that point in my life.

So we found a four-bedroom house on twenty-five acres of land that we could rent; it was huge! Plus, there was so much land for the kids to play around in, and there was a river or creek that ran through it; it was perfect. Each kid would have their own room, and there was enough room that I did not have to see my husband if I wanted to. We moved in immediately after we found out through the property owner that three hundred applicants applied to rent this house, and we were the ones to get it. Coincidence? I think not.

While we were moving into this house, my eldest son, who was now thirteen, was moving stuff down in the basement when suddenly he came running upstairs so fast, tripping on the last step and falling. He was screaming at the top of his lungs, "We have to move!" I had never seen him look so scared in my life. And I asked him why. And he told me that there was a tombstone in the basement.

I said, "A tombstone?"

"Yes!"

So my husband and I went down to the basement to see it, and my eldest son was right; there was a full tombstone down there, leaning up against the wall, but the strange thing about it was that the last name on the tombstone was our last name, Taylor. Freaky! It did freak us out, and we thought, "Is this why the property owner rented it to us?" LOL. I did not understand why they did not remove that tombstone before anyone moved in. We just did not think anything about it. I know you're probably thinking this shit only happens in movies, right? I'm telling you this is a true story.

After we moved in, I was working six days a week and focusing on taking care of my kids. I did not want them to go without anything. They were my life; everything that I did was for them.

My husband and I were still having issues in our relationship, and I was working as much as I could to avoid him, so I wanted to keep myself busy to not be around him. In my spare time, I decided that I wanted to become an EMT. I volunteered at our local firehouse and got to know the firefighters and EMTs, and they wanted to sponsor me to go to college and become an EMT-basic. I loved doing that type of work; helping people was where my passion started to come in. I started to realize there is more to life than myself and my problems. It was my new escape to get out of the fucked-up world that I was living in.

After one year in college, I took my practical and became an EMT. Besides the birth of my children, that was one of the biggest accomplishments I had in my life. I was starting to feel like my life had a purpose; I mean, I knew it had a purpose because I was raising three kids.

One weekend my husband took the kids to spend time at his brother's house, and I was at the house, just enjoying the peace and alone time. I decided to log onto the internet and go into the chat rooms; it was a fantastic way to meet new people, and I loved the different people with whom I was chatting. The date was May 24, 2004. Unexpectedly, while I was in this chat room, a woman came across, messaging me; her name was Jessica.

4

The Psychic

My conversation with Jessica went as follows word for word:

Jessica: Hi, my name is Jessica, where are you from?

Me: I am from Williston, and you? [Williston was the town I lived in at the time.]

Jessica: New Mexico. I used to live in Essex. [Essex was a town next to Williston.]

Jessica: I left because I was in the wrong kind of work for Vermont.

Me: Really? What do you do for work?

Jessica: I am glad you asked. I tried to start a psychic hotline. B4 you ignore me, let me prove to you that I am psychic.

Me: Gee go for it!

Jessica: As you smirk and say she is full of shit.

Jessica: Ask me a question about you and I will tell you the answer.

Jessica: Humor me?

Jessica: Mona is it??

Me: Duh?

Jessica: Rather good, huh? Now, ask me something good about you and I will tell you!

Jessica: Like your Birthday, 02/05/1964….

Jessica: How am I doing?

Me: You are the psychic, you should know!

Jessica: ?

Me: Wrong!

At this point I was freaking out. I did not know who this woman was and what she wanted from me. I did not know if someone was playing a game with me. I did not know what was going on, so I did not feed her any information. But I was thinking, "How does she know my name and my birth date? But I continued to play dumb.

JESSICA: And you have the look on your face that tells me you are lying.

ME: I do not lie.

JESSICA: How about the fact that your Birthday signifies another, Wait…. Two birthdays in your family with the same Birthday.

JESSICA: Wrong again??

ME: You're right.

At this point I was freaking out; this woman was spot on! I have a twin brother, and my adopted brother was born on our seventh birthday! How did she know this about me? Was she a stalker? Was I being punked? I did not know what was going on here.

JESSICA: Closer to home, in the following order by age, K, J, T, & M....

JESSICA: J and T may be wrong, but close.

ME: I do not know a K or a T.

JESSICA: Ken

JESSICA: Terry

JESSICA: whoooooow!

JESSICA: She is good!

JESSICA: Am I right?

ME: Maybe?

Again, she was spot on, and I was shaking at this point.

JESSICA: Maybe means, yes, but with hesitation.

JESSICA: You should not smoke when you are nervous!

ME: I am not!

At this point I was looking around my house, outside my windows, and outside my house because I felt like someone was watching me.

JESSICA: Marlboro, is it?

ME: Wrong again!

JESSICA: I also sense a change in your job status recently.

JESSICA: you left a big company for many varied reasons.
JESSICA: Can I share something with you?? The main reason you left.
ME: OK who are you, Jessica?
ME: Sure
JESSICA: you are leaving these jobs which, has not been the first time you have left a job, because of the way your parents treated you growing up. Specifically, your mother. However, your father had a lot of influence on you as well.
ME: No that was not the reason at all!
JESSICA: I said one of the reasons.
ME: Your off base!
I thought my reason for quitting that job was the married man I was having an affair with. I could not take being around him anymore, and I wanted to move on with my life.
ME: That was not even one.
JESSICA: Not the fact that your boss would not give you overtime, or the working conditions sucked, or the hours you worked were just the opposite of the man you are with…
JESSICA: Not off base now, am I??
ME: I am not with a man.
ME: Who are you and why did you pick me to chat with?
JESSICA: No, the real reason you keep leaving is because

of that insecure feeling you have because your father yelled all the time.

JESSICA: I picked you because I want to help.

JESSICA: I want you to smile more.

JESSICA: I want you to have that feeling you used to have when you were growing up at Christmas.

JESSICA: I want you to know that you are an incredibly special person!

ME: I know I am!

JESSICA: I want you to know that you ARE an incredibly special person!!

JESSICA: Good

JESSICA: And you say you do not lie, and I agree, you are not technically with a man, you just share expenses.

ME: True

JESSICA: I sense a few relative changes, like your job situation, from job-to-job, uneasiness…Marriages. 3?

ME: Yes

JESSICA: First R, then M, then L, now T??

ME: How do you know this?? [How did she know my last name? These were all the initials of my last names!] this is getting to be too much!

JESSICA: And I am not even charging you anything. You have been charged by other psychics in the past, haven't you?

JESSICA: I sense that

ME: just one

JESSICA: I see it in my mind.

JESSICA: I feel what she said

ME: I have not really got into them.

JESSICA: Not good news she gave you

ME: what is that?

JESSICA: news that did come true

JESSICA: IT was at a fair, true?

ME: I do not know what you are talking about!

ME: or else I blocked it out of my mind!

JESSICA: Do not get upset…. Promise?

JESSICA: you blocked it out.

ME: I will not, I promise.

JESSICA: B… [Billy]

ME: what about him?

JESSICA: A psychic told you that he would not be with you, in body, forever.

JESSICA: whoops

ME: yes, she did.

ME: and he is not!

JESSICA: you blocked it.

JESSICA: I sense that

JESSICA: but that was years ago, and he is still with you, in spirit every day. He plays with M, when you hear

M talking and playing by himself and talking to someone.

JESSICA: every day

ME: Huh?

JESSICA: Who is M? You do not have to tell me, but he is your son who lives with you. Mic, Mark, Max, Michael??

JESSICA: incredibly young. Well, young. Walking and talking anyway.

She named my son.

ME: my son

JESSICA: your son?

JESSICA: TY

JESSICA: Do you believe in angels?

ME: I just find all of this too strange.

ME: Yes, I do believe in angels!

JESSICA: you have an incredibly special purpose. You do not know it and you can try to make all the changes in your life with your search for material things, but you do not need these things. Even cosmetic changes to yourself…I sense recently.

ME: Yes [I had breast implants put in because I lost a lot of weight, and I did it for cosmetic reasons.]

JESSICA: You do not need stuff. You have been sent here for service. By someone very loving, someone that loves you very much. I know this does not make much sense right now, but it will. Even by the end of this year. It will!!

JESSICA: make amends with loved ones that you were not having a good relationship with. I sense you have started a healing process with an exceedingly difficult relationship.

JESSICA: Yes, you did, and it was in May so, I could guess and say it was with your mother?

JESSICA: Mother's Day.

JESSICA: Your mother.

JESSICA: Let me tell you what I just felt about your mother.

JESSICA: R U there or am I freakin' you out?

ME: I am here

JESSICA: Are you, ok?

ME: So far, you're right.

ME: Yes, I am fine, I just find this very weird, that is all, to have someone I do not know, know so much about my life!

JESSICA: Your life, my life, everyone's life is together.

JESSICA: light, love, all feed from the same pool.

ME: And why did you pick me out of the whole chat room?

ME: true!

JESSICA: Do you believe in angels?

JESSICA: Huh?

Me: Yes, I do!

Jessica: Good

Jessica: Your mother has some things locked in her mind. Not all good. She battles with a very, exceedingly elevated level of intelligence and psychic energy that is bottled in her mind because her father would do the same that your father would do… Yell and scream and swear and take the Lord's name in vain.

Me: Very True

Jessica: Her mind is racing. "Lay there at night and my mind won't stop."

Jessica: I sense she has said this b4?

Me: Yes, she has, I am the same way.

Jessica: she is battling with all this "Stuff." Let her be free. Love her for who she is and her worries (how everyone views her) will slowly go away.

Jessica: P… [She dropped four names, and one of them was my grandfather's name.]

Jessica: He was abusive

Me: my grandfather

Jessica: He was a pig

Me: yes, he was

Jessica: and he had sex with your aunt…

Jessica: there, damn it, I said it!

Me: Yes, I knew that

JESSICA: oh, okay

ME: This is just too weird!

JESSICA: Do not judge her, she is filled with guilt as well. You have a brother…I just keep seeing a repeat name, so, I will say it as I hear it. [Then she named my father, my brother, and my brother's son. They are all the same.]

JESSICA: three of the same names

ME: oh my god yes! My brother, father, and nephew!

JESSICA: Incredibly special people

JESSICA: They are still linked because your dad is gone, I am sorry, is this true?

JESSICA: Your Dad?

ME: Yes

JESSICA: they are very linked, oh my word, very linked

JESSICA: Your brother has been given a special gift from your dad

JESSICA: Was your brother there when your father died?

ME: yes, he was

JESSICA: oh, my word, yes

JESSICA: he was

ME: yes

JESSICA: you just finished my sentence

JESSICA: Your brother carries the gift of sight.

ME: he says he does

JESSICA: and anyone that he touches, not just physically, will have the gift.

JESSICA: If they listen

JESSICA: His son, wow!! His gift is extraordinarily strong and will grow.

JESSICA: Sorry back to your mother

ME: OK

JESSICA: Your brother was there when your father died. That is how I started on your brother.

ME: Yes

JESSICA: and your mother is full of guilt

JESSICA: she waited too long to call anyone

ME: oh my god!

JESSICA: I feel I may be wrong.

ME: no, you are not!

JESSICA: Do not judge your mother

ME: OK

JESSICA: She wanted the pain of her relationship gone

JESSICA: They did not get along

JESSICA: I sense your father was not in the best of health.

JESSICA: Self-indulgence

ME: You're right

JESSICA: Three things

JESSICA: Food, TV, video games, or computer

JESSICA: Do not really know about the last one.

JESSICA: I am leaning toward the computer

JESSICA: IBM?

ME: You are so on the money

JESSICA: Do you believe in angels?

ME: Yes, I do

JESSICA: Good

JESSICA: at any rate, your mom's relationship ended, so she thought when your dad died.

JESSICA: your brother did not revive your dad, so he thinks.

JESSICA: Your father released his gift to him then. It just seemed like he revived him.

ME: you are so right! My sister and she let him die.

JESSICA: He is still in her mind. She still calls him dad.

JESSICA: Sister thank you, another special girl

JESSICA: bad luck with men though

ME: yes

JESSICA: similar relationship as you

JESSICA: Man in the house, shares the bills, sex occasionally

ME: yes again.

JESSICA: he cheated on her recently.

ME: Yes

JESSICA: she just had some surgery like you…Yours was cosmetic, hers necessary.

ME: yes

JESSICA: a joint. Leg surgery?? Did she have leg surgery?

ME: yes, her knee

JESSICA: right knee?

ME: yes again

JESSICA: she needs the other done, you know? She is in denial and does not sit well so she will put it Off.

JESSICA: she is also stuck on this silly search for material things

ME: Yes, she knows this

JESSICA: All these material things will not matter on your day of judgment.

JESSICA: Trust me

JESSICA: you will look back and say, in your words, "Why the fuck did I chase all that shit!"

JESSICA: Smile

JESSICA: You know it

ME: Yes, I am at that point in life.

ME: so again, I ask why did you pick me today?

JESSICA: Do not worry. Live in the here and now. Take this new venture you have started. Put your heart and soul into it. But do not get so engrossed in it that you cannot enjoy a smile.

JESSICA: you cannot enjoy your two sons....You have lost more than one. Oh, I am SO sorry!

ME: Yes, I have

JESSICA: Justin?

ME: Yes, oh my god.

JESSICA: God is with you and him. I sense a strong boy,

> Justin. Looks remarkably like his twin, however, he is not laden with flesh, he talks clearly and laughs a lot. He will be with his twin forever and help him through tough times.

Me: Oh my god this is just too weird and right on the money!

Me: I have never had anyone know all of this about me! It is blowing my mind right now!

Jessica: I must go for now. You asked repeatedly, "why you pick me today?" I have answered you over and over. You must have faith. Trust, love, and listen to simple things like the sound of the wind in the trees, only then will you believe. Do you believe in angels?

Me: yes

Jessica: good

Me: ok thanks and I will talk to you again soon

Jessica: We will speak again. I am with you. Call your mom this weekend. Just so you will believe, I have a slight corner of my heart that is being pulled

Jessica: he loved watching you grow up

Me: who?

Jessica: He loved talking with you

Jessica: He loved being around you

Jessica: He loved watching you wreck his car!

Me: MY DAD!

Jessica: He is bringing you to the roller-skating rink.

Me: YES!

Jessica: He especially loved skating with you during couples.

Me: YES!

Jessica: He is strong, and he watches you!

Jessica: He loves you!

Jessica: Squeeze Bucket

Me: Hey! He called my sister that!

Jessica: Okay. Wrong Sister.

Jessica: [She then mentioned the pet name my dad always called me.]

Jessica: He may be strong, but he forgets to.

Me: This is so strange! But it is all right!

Jessica: That was funny. I feel him laughing!

Jessica: strong laugh!

Jessica: Do you believe in angels?

Me: Yes!

Jessica: good

Where did that come from? Who was this woman? And why was she coming to me during this time in my life? Was this divine intervention? I had not been much of a spiritual person up to this point in my life, and I just did not know what to make of this encounter. How could a stranger know so much about me and my family and my life and have so many details—birthdays, last names, relationships? I did not know what to think about all this.

I could not sleep for a couple of days because all I thought about was that conversation with Jessica. I was logging on and off the computer, hoping to talk with her again. I was so intrigued. But there was nothing until three days later.

5

The Psychic and the Chakras?

I logged onto the computer again, and I went into the chat rooms. The day was May 27, 2004. And the conversation went as follows:

Jessica: A watched pot never boils.

Me: What?

Jessica: A watched pot; it never boils.

Me: I do not understand.

Jessica: You have been looking for me??

Me: Yes, I have

Jessica: Things you want hardly ever come to you when you want but when you least expect it.

Jessica: A watched pot never boils.

Me: Yes, I understand this.

Jessica: How are you?

Me: I am fine and you?

Jessica: Good

Jessica: Go ahead and ask

Me: I just found it strange. I talked to my brother the other day and he told me that he dreamt about our conversation the other day.

Me: He knew who you were.

Jessica: I met him once

Jessica: he is big-time into channeling.

Me: Yes, he is, I found it odd

Jessica: a flirt too

Me: lol

Jessica: Big flirt, like his dad??

Me: very much so

Me: I found it odd the day you talked to me, and he knew everything that you and I had discussed, he knew your name and everything before I even mentioned it.

Jessica: We talked in his dream. He goes a lot to the place where your grandparents are buried.

Me: Yes, he does he live in that area, he said you were in his dream with my father, he knows what you look like, and he thinks your cute. lol

Jessica: Yes, stop thinking so much that this is weird, think of it as a blessing, I cannot speak with you in this form for long. The way things are aligned, allow it. This will not be for much longer.

Jessica: You need to change some things in your life. Not many. Some

Me: I do think of it as a blessing, I consider you my guardian angel! This is a reason for this, I feel it.

Jessica: Your Guardian Angel is not me. She is, as you would say, "in training." However, has been linked to you for a purpose.

Jessica: She will make herself more evident to you when you change things. Right now, your energies are not aligned properly and will not allow you to converse with her.

Jessica: I know…WHAT??

Jessica: What does that mean???

Me: I do not know how to align my energies though.

Jessica: Let me tell you the changes you should make that will align you better.

Jessica: okay?

Me: Please???

Jessica: Sure

Jessica: You need to become familiar with your Chakras. Have you heard of these?

Me: No, I have not

Jessica: I know you have seen them

Me: I have heard my siblings talk about them.

Jessica: The old wife's tale of, "At the end of the rainbow is a pot of gold." Ever hear this?

Me: Yes, I have

Jessica: Light, Love, the pursuit of happiness?? Ever heard of this?

Me: oh yes! Lol, that is me! Looking for

Jessica: I felt your laughter

Me: Yes

Jessica: They are all one entity.

Me: I agree with you

Jessica: Light, Love, happiness, and the rainbow

Jessica: to express how that relates to the Chakras…

Me: Go on

Jessica: I will give you some homework, is that fair?

Me: Very fair. I love homework! lol

Jessica: This may seem weird, however, here goes

Me: ok

Jessica: Roy G. Biv. Do you know of this person?

Me: No, I do not, he does not sound familiar

Jessica: It is the colors of the rainbow. Red, Orange, Yellow, Green, Blue, Indigo, Violet.

Jessica: Each color is on the visible spectrum of light.

Me: Yes

Jessica: Each aligned with every part of your body. Every day!!

Jessica: I know. Red, Defensiveness, Moody, Anger, Diabetes, Bad Relationship with Mom, and bad Knees.

Jessica: Orange; Appetite, Sexual Drive

Jessica: Yellow; Ego

Jessica: Green; Age of the fallacy of the heart's color as red. Psychics see it as Green.

Me: Yes

Jessica: Blue; Self Expression

Jessica: Indigo; Your Nephew's color…The gift of sight.

Me: and my brother

Jessica: Violet; Higher Self, Soul

Me: Yes

Jessica: At any rate, if your chakras are blocked, and for example the fourth chakra is green, you would love easy. You will be distant.

Jessica: First Chakra, Red. You will be in a bad mood a lot, Depressed, Anxious, and Hypertension.

Me: That is me!

Jessica: The pills you took a few months ago did not work because your base chakra is locked up.

Me: Yes, you are right, I do not take them anymore.

Jessica: You became angry, recluse, distant.

Me: very much so, worse off.

Jessica: That is because the wrong doctor treated you. Example: Ritalin for "Busy" kids. What a joke.

> Medical doctors give medicine, Spiritual Doctors fix the Chakras!

Jessica: It is like putting a band-aid on a crushed skull

Jessica: stops the bleeding but...

Me: I agree with you, I did not want to temporarily solve the problem or mask it, I wanted to solve it!

Jessica: Right so...Homework.

Me: Lol

Jessica: Listen to the trees, I will bet you have gone for walks, I feel this, excellent job.

Me: yes, I have

Jessica: you had an uncle named after the trees. Great man, I am sure.

Me: I am thinking. [After thinking a little bit, I realized the name of my grandfather's brother was Forest.]

Jessica: Learn about Chakras and you will start to hear You and your, as you call it, guardian angel. We call it a spirit guide.

Me: I will most definitely do that!

Jessica: a book is great. Gets you out of the house. Gives you something to look forward to. Makes you feel, in a way, like Xmas again! Excitement!!!

Me: Lol you are so right! It is like you see my life! I wish I could lol

Jessica: Do not let our conversation get you hypertension and miss SLEEP, did we??

Jessica: yes, you did

Me: OMG yes.

Jessica: A clear mind is worth everything.

Me: I need one

Jessica: I will collaborate with you to clear your mind

Me: LOL

Jessica: Yes

Me: Thank you! There is a reason for everything.

Jessica: You will feel better soon. Yes, there is, I will show you. By the end of the year, I will not be able to communicate with you, so, we have work to do.

Jessica: Does he think I am cute? Well, I will have to get him going in the next dream. Lol

Me: he knew everything

Jessica: He will not cross the line. He loves his wife because his mind is clear.

Me: Which sent chills through my spine.

Jessica: flirt, yes...

Jessica: Chills

Me: Yes, he says he clears his mind before he goes to bed each night

Jessica: Do not confuse your "Chills" with anything other than your body trying to be intuitive.

Me: No, it was a good feeling

Jessica: Yes, it is

Jessica: It is Psychic!!

Jessica: Trust me

Me: yes

Jessica: That's how I know

Jessica: When I am right about something.

Jessica: Chiles

Jessica: Yes right, chilis. I go to lunch at Chili's

Me: LOL

Jessica: Chills, Darn it!!!

Me: WOW

Jessica: So, your mind is intellect. And…Your chills are intuition.

Jessica: If we can clear your mind and keep the chills coming, we will be hitting one thousand!

Jessica: Lol

Me: That is my goal!

Jessica: Just like when I ask you if you believe in Angels, I will say, Good!

Jessica: I must go for now. One more thing?

Jessica: Actually, two more things

Me: Just do my homework and learn about Chakras?

Jessica: No, two more additional things

Me: what is that?

Jessica: One, I have a feeling when you are online, so when I have "Stuff" to tell you, I will find you. You do not have to look for me. OKAY?

Me: Okay I will not

Jessica: Good. Lastly

Me: I knew that for some reason

Jessica: I knew you did

Jessica: Lastly, and I am sorry, but her name will not come into my mind other than what you and he told me, squeeze bucket.

Jessica: Do not tell me

Jessica: I need to keep my skills sharp, and it will come to me.

Jessica: I see her clearly, however.

Jessica: nice girl!

Me: My sister is squeeze bucket

Jessica: looks a lot like me only, Sorry squeeze bucket, is a little thicker.

Me: Lol

Jessica: I know your sister is squeeze bucket, I just need to think of her name. I will ask your brother if he is channeling tonight.

Jessica: Anyway

Jessica: She will, if she has not already, start some changes this week, she may THINK they are MAJOR changes, but tell her to trust in the Lord and keep praying. He hears all her prayers.

Me: I have told her

Jessica: They are not major. Just necessary. Like her knee. Tell her that I said she needs to listen to you, my newest apprentice, and her brother. Smile; do not cry. Laugh, do not think, be with her friend…M HEY!! I got it. I was thinking M&M. [My sister's name starts with an M, and so does her best friend's name.] I love how it works! Tell your sister and her friend to have fun!

Jessica: Okay?

Me: You are so right, that is my sister and her best friend! I will tell her.

Jessica: Okay. I must go. Until next time.

Me: Bye Jessica and I will do my homework as you asked!

Jessica: OHHHHHH!! One more thing. Tell your brother that everything will come to a close, and Uncle Sam will be good with him by the end of August!! BYE

Me: I will. Bye for now!

I did not know who this woman was or where she had come from, but I loved talking to her. She had started to open my eyes to a whole new perspective in life.

The minute I finished talking to her online, I ran to the nearest Barnes & Noble bookstore and wanted to find every book I could on chakras. I never knew what chakras were, and I had never heard of them before. I bought my first chakra book. It was called *The Book of Chakras*. I read that book from front to cover and learned so much about the energy centers that surround our bodies.

After I finished that book, I went and bought more books on chakras. I wanted to get the full perspective of what they were all about. These conversations with Jessica started my whole spiritual journey in life. I finally felt like this was going to help me become more balanced and grounded. I had been through so much, and these conversations—I do not care what anybody says—were divine interventions to me, and I was going to take full advantage of this opportunity. I did have conversations with my sister and my brother about these discussions with Jessica, but I did not want to tell anyone else about them because I did not want them to think that I was crazy.

6

Putting the Pieces Together

I started to dive deep into these conversations. I printed them off my computer, and I was reading everything that we said to each other with a fine-tooth comb. A lot of things that Jessica said stood out to me. What did she mean I left jobs because of the way my parents treated me growing up, specifically my mother? However, my father had a lot of influence on me as well. I could not understand what she meant by my mother. I did not have a relationship with her. She did not inspire me or teach me anything about being a woman. I could not communicate with her; I felt like she did not care or was not even interested in what I had to say. So when Jessica said specifically, "Your mother," it perplexed me. I picked that statement apart until I was blue in the face. So again, I thought the most positive role model in any child's life is the parent of the same sex.

Then she said the real reason I left was the insecurity I had because my father yelled and screamed all the time. That statement I understood completely, but I never thought that that was the reason I was leaving jobs a lot. I thought I was leaving because I was not growing or evolving anymore in these companies. I was not advancing in positions. Then I suddenly got an aha moment. Did I leave these jobs because I could not communicate with my coworkers and bosses? Was it because I did not care about what others said at work? Was I not inspiring or teaching any of my coworkers (my mother)? And did it scare me when my boss (my father) would yell or get mad? Was I getting into all these unhealthy relationships with men because I was insecure about myself? I realized that I had no self-worth because I was not taught it! These were the pieces of the puzzle that I was putting together.

Then she told me twice that I was a *very* special person and that I had a very, very special purpose. Then she said, "You have been sent here for service." Was she trying to tell me something that I did not know? I had always been a very inquisitive person. Was I reading too much into that statement? Or was I supposed to figure out what my purpose was in life? I am telling you, she said she wanted to help me clear my mind, but she was making me think of more questions that I wanted to ask because I was so curious.

Jessica validated a few things that I was thinking about when she told me about my grandfather sleeping with my grandmother's sister and when she mentioned that my mother waited too long to call for help when my father passed away. I was so shocked to hear this! I knew my mother waited too long because she called me after it happened and told me that my father had fallen to the floor, and she did not know what to do, so I told her to call 911. Thirty minutes later I called her back, and she said that she had not called them yet, and she called 411 instead.

Jessica said that my mother had things locked in her mind, and they were not good. She battled with an extremely elevated level of intelligence and psychic energy that was bottled in her mind because her father did the same things that my father would do—yell and scream and swear and take the Lord's name in vain. Was Jessica telling me that her childhood was abusive with her father, and it was also abusive with my father? That was why she waited so long to call for help with my father. I questioned these things because it did not justify letting someone die. After all, you chose not to get out of an abusive relationship.

Jessica was telling me that she was battling with all this "stuff," and she wanted me to let her be free, love her for who she is and her worries, and not judge her for her actions like my grandfather and father did. How can you forgive someone for their actions when they let someone die and chose not to do anything about it? Is that not the most selfish act that one can do? I mean, I did not have the greatest relationship with my father, but who does this in life?

It was a wonder she was battling with some "stuff." I would be too! Your mother was full of guilt because she wanted the pain of her relationship gone; they did not get along. And your dad was not in the best of health, meaning self-indulgence. My father weighed 450 lb. and lived to eat; he did not eat to live.

Jessica had asked me several times if I believed in angels, and I did not know why she kept asking me that question. I started thinking. After everything that I had experienced in my life so far at the age of forty-five, I must have a lot of angels around me, or I would. I then began researching angels and spirit guides.

When all this was happening, my husband and I were fighting so much and not getting along, and his daughter decided to move out on her own. About a year after his daughter moved out, she called me up and said, "Hey, I have someone I want you to meet." She came over to my house and introduced me to her newborn son! I was like, "What!" There is disconnection with someone when you do not see them for at least a year, they have a baby, and you do not even know that they have been pregnant. What the hell! She was eighteen years old. It reminded me of my mother not knowing she was pregnant with twins. I started to see so many patterns from the past repeating themselves in my life.

At this point I needed a major overhaul. I decided to quit my job because even though the affair that I had with that man at work was over, I just could not see him every day at work. I ended up getting another job that paid more money and better health benefits. In one week, I separated from my husband, got a new job, and moved into my new rented condominium. I wanted to break all the patterns of abuse and fighting and arguing from my past and not have them in my future. I had three failed marriages, and I was done with trying to have any relationship with anyone. I needed to do this to figure out what was important in my life. I wanted to be happy, and that was all I wanted for him too, and it was quite evident that we were not making each other happy. I wanted the best for him.

After about four years in my rented condominium, I was doing a lot of work on myself, becoming more aware of who I was and who I was becoming. I was managing my emotions, and I was doing a lot of self-reflection and inner work. I was working on my chakras. I started meditating and reading any self-help books I could get my hands on, from Doreen Virtue to Tony Robbins, Esther Hicks, Bob Proctor, Dr. Wayne Dyer, and so on. I even started taking a lot of online classes with these people to become more self-aware and focused. I was starting to realize that everyone in life makes mistakes, and how else are we supposed to learn in life if we do not make any mistakes?

I was curious to see if marriage could come back stronger when both people cheated on each other. Jessica and my studying made me realize that I cannot judge people for their behavior because their behaviors are not who that person is. And we should not judge someone if we have not walked a day in their shoes. No one knows what someone else is going through in their life unless you have a conversation with them to understand.

Jessica and the above people put me on a spiritual journey of self-discovery and had me ask deeper questions in life, such as Why am I here? Why am I going through all this in my life? Who am I? And why do I act the way I act and behave the way I behave?

For years I struggled with depression, anger, and lack of faith. When Billy and Justin passed away, that took a toll on me, how I acted, and how I behaved. I was a serious manic-depressive. There were a couple of times I wanted to take my own life (I was working as an armed guard, delivering money to banks at the time, and I had a loaded gun locked up in the house at all times), and I could easily have done that to myself. But I could not do that to my kids? I loved them too much, and I could not put them through that. My kids had always been my driving force to pull me through anything that I was going through. I had a deeper feeling that there was something bigger than what I was going through, and

I always felt that way. I always felt like God would not put me on this earth to go through all this bullshit for nothing. There was a reason why I was going through all this.

Even though my third ex-husband and I were divorced, he had always been a great friend and confidant to me and had been there for me even during our divorce. No matter what mood I was in, high or low, he stood by my side. That man busted his ass off to build trust with me again. I mean, there were times that I was the biggest bitch to him, and he never once got mad at me or said anything; he just let me say and do my thing. Did I think, "Hmm, this man is here for me until the end"? I started to see him from an unfamiliar perspective. So we had a lengthy conversation and decided to give our relationship one more chance.

But I was getting to the point where I just could not stand being depressed or mad or angry anymore; I did not like the feeling, and I did not like myself being this way. I wanted to take charge of my feelings and emotions without taking any pills or antidepressants or being labeled with a mental illness like my grandmother and my mother. I wanted to break all the patterns from my past and not bring them into my future. When the kids were young, yes, I did yell and scream a lot. I am not justifying that it was right, but I never once laid a hand on them. I never hit them or spanked them at all. But the yelling and screaming was still there. It was there for my mother when she was growing up as a child, it was there for me when I was growing up as a child, and then I was doing it to my children. This must stop!

I had been in my rented condominium for six years, and my property owner told me that I had to move because her grandfather owned it, and he had passed away. So she gave me a month to find another place. "Who gives anyone a month to find another place?" I thought. I was at the point in my life where I was sick and tired of renting, and I wanted to buy my own place. I was forty-six years old, and I had never owned my own place yet. I was searching high and low for a place of my own, so I found one. I bought a condominium in the same development but in a different parking lot. LOL. I loved the location. It was close to all amenities, and it was five minutes away from my job, so it was perfect. This was the first time that I owned a place! I was excited.

So at this point in our lives, my ex-husband's daughter and my son were twenty years old, they have moved out of the house, and my stepdaughter had had another child, who was a girl. My youngest son was twelve, so we had two grandchildren at this point, whom we spoiled as much as possible, especially at Christmastime. I love the look on children's faces at Christmas; that is where I get all my joy from. It brings tears to my eyes.

I must admit now that I am grown, and when I look back at my childhood, the best memory that I have in my life is

Christmas. Christmas growing up was my father's favorite time of the year, and he always would make sure the family was together with kids and grandchildren. I miss those days. I felt closest to him before he passed and during the holidays. That was the only thing that I copied from my past and brought forward in my life, the closeness of family during the holidays. Everything else I left behind.

Every Christmas my sister and my mother would spend time with my younger brother and his wife. They never spent time with me and my family at Christmas, and I could never understand why. I would notice that my mother would buy presents for my kids, and then she stopped doing it because I was told they never thanked her. I would see her buy gifts for her boyfriend's older kids but not her grandchildren! "Who fuckin' does this?" I was thinking. "What grandmother does not spend time with her grandkids and not buy them any gifts at Christmastime?"

And I noticed that my sister did not want to spend much time with my sons. My sons would always ask me what they did. My sister was not married; she had been divorced and single for about fifteen years! And she did not have any children in her life. She told me that she did not want to have any children because babysitting us when she was a child scared her. I always felt sorry for her, having that responsibility at such a young age to take care of four other kids. I could never imagine ever not having any kids in my lifetime!

They bring so much joy and experience to one's life; you learn so much from them, so many different perspectives. My children have taught me so much in life: love, patience, compassion, empathy, just to name a few. I can see things differently in life through such a diverse set of eyes. I could never imagine not leaving a part of myself behind in this world when I am gone. My kids are my legacy.

I also observed over the years that my sister was trying so desperately to have any type of relationship with my mother, but she could not. My sister would call me up so frustrated about all the things that my mother did or said, and she would constantly complain about her behavior. Now just to let you know, my mother was seventy-five years old at this point in her life. She was still clever; she still remembered dates and a lot of things in her life. She still had all her faculties. My sister would tell me that my mother would be incontinent in her Depend undergarments and not change them. She would smell like urine. And my sister would yell and scream at her for it. She would say, "Do you not know you're pissing in your pants and you smell like urine?"

I would think, "Who would yell and scream at an elderly person for incontinence? Who are you to talk to her like that?" Could she not accept my mother for who she was and what she was doing? At that age, she was not going to change.

After I moved out of my mother's house, I did not have a close relationship with her because I knew and learned that she was not emotionally or mentally there. I observed them meticulously over the years and heard all the things that my sister was doing to try to have a relationship with her. I would have conversations with my mother on the phone, but I would just listen to her and be cordial, then hang up. I would not get mad at her; I just accepted her for who she was. Jessica taught me that. I knew at her age that if she wanted to change her behavior, she would already have done so. But I came to realize she was who she was; she was not going to change, and that was that. I learned to let go of all emotional and mental attachments to her, and I felt good about it and comfortable with it.

My sister, on the other hand, tried desperately to have any type of relationship with her, and it really hurt to watch. My mother would get sick and tired of hearing the frustration in my sister; she would comment, "Well, anyways!" This was what my sister would tell me. When I thought about what Jessica said, it made so much sense. That was my mother's way of changing the subject with my sister because she did not want to hear her complain anymore about what she was doing. My mother was yelled and screamed at by her father her whole life, and then when she married my dad, she heard him yelling and screaming all the time. She thought she finally got rid of the yelling and screaming in her life when my dad passed away, but she did not because my sister took over and started doing it with her. And now that I thought about it,

I didn't have a great relationship with my sister because she was doing it to me! Whoo! Light-bulb moment! OK, here was another pattern I must work on from my past—my sister.

7

My Sister

My sister and I had had many issues in our lives, and we had not had that close of a relationship growing up. My whole life I had never had close relationships with women. I started to become aware of this; it probably stemmed from not having good role models in my life. I had to start working on this as well. I came to realize that it was so easy for me to hang around men for several reasons: I wanted to know how men ticked because my dad was so abusive, I wanted to learn why they did the things they did when they were in relationships, and men were so much easier to talk to without judgment. I did not want the cattiness, the competition, the jealousy, the fighting and arguing, and the judgment as I saw with my mom and my sister and other women. You just do not get any of that from men when it comes to friendship.

My sister was very education driven and into her career because she was single. I saw her going after material things—a nice car, a nice house, and her diplomas. (She had associate and bachelor's degrees; I am so proud of her!) I wanted a family and a loving relationship over career. I am so proud of everything that she has accomplished in her life. I could see that we were two completely different people with our wants and needs. What is good for one is not necessarily good for another; we each have our paths to follow in life, and I believe these differences caused a lot of our disagreements in the past. Love, to me, was more important than a career because, as Jessica previously said, on your day of judgment, having all these material things is not going to matter. I started to realize that I would always have the memories of love with me but not how well I did at my job. If I died tomorrow, my job would replace me in a heartbeat; but as a mother, if I died tomorrow, my kids could never replace me.

Things started to shift in my perspective. There were a lot of times growing up when I felt like my sister could not see through my perspective, and we would fight a lot. I never wanted to spend time with her and my mother at the same time because it gave me the chills just being around them both together, and those chills were not good. I saw that they just fought all the time. I was being shown by my sister and my mother that women just don't have a good relationship with each other. I just did not see them inspiring each other or lifting each other up as women.

I started to notice that my sister and her best friend were getting along the same way as my mother and sister. I started to see the cattiness, the competition, the jealousy, the fighting and arguing, and the judgment with these women. I noticed the body language of each and the tone in their voices, and I was hearing the comments made back and forth to each other; some of them were very sharp and abrasive. But then again that was my perspective. You feel that stuff intensely when you are a highly empathic person. My sister's friend was up at her house, visiting her; her friend would do her dishes and clean her kitchen and come out on the patio to let my sister know what she had done, and my sister would comment, "It's like she needs validation on everything that she does!"

I was like, "*What?* Can you not thank her for cleaning your kitchen for you? And if she does want validation, is there anything wrong with that? If you are thinking that she needs validation, then that is your soul telling you to give it to her! Maybe she does not receive validation at home or work or from her boyfriend, and she is at least hoping she can get some from her best friend." Maybe I just think differently, I do not know. Why am I seeing my sister like this?

My sister would tell me all the reasons why she did not like her friend's boyfriend. She was worried that he was an alcoholic, and he smoked pot all the time. (Smoking pot in our state is legal, just to let you know). And she did not think that he was good enough for her. I could understand that she had concern for her friend; my sister had the biggest heart of gold when it came to helping people and being concerned about their welfare, or at least I thought that was the case. I soon realized that my sister only did things for other people if it benefited her in some way; she had to get something out of anything that she did for anyone.

But her friend was sixty-two years old and old enough to make her own decisions. This was what she felt was best for her right now on her life path; who were we to judge? I was also thinking, "You smoke pot just like he does, but it is not OK for him to do it with her. So are you also saying that it's not right that you are doing it as well if you see that it is not right for others?" I thought that was very hypocritical.

I started noticing that my sister would talk to my sister-in-law the same way. I saw the cattiness, the competition, and the sharp comments made to each other, especially when they were having a few drinks. I would see them try to one-up each other on their jobs. Who was more superior? In the end does it really matter? And who are we trying to impress here?

I'm very aware of the patterns here because I have trained myself to become very mindful of my surroundings and people's behaviors, actions, body language, and so forth. I spent well over three years studying all these things. I also started noticing that she copied a lot of the things that my brother and his wife and I would buy. For example, if I mentioned to her that I was reading a book, she would buy it. My brother and his wife bought alarm systems for their house; she went out and bought the same system. I told her that I bought a safety-deposit box, and she went out and bought the same one. She bought the same incense that I used; she went out and replaced her appliances in her kitchen when my brother and his wife did. And the list went on and on. I think she was not an innovator; she was an imitator!

I had to question myself, "Why am I innately seeing these things within her? Why am I seeing these behaviors in her but not in other women?"

I would ask her about these things, and she would say, "If someone in our family has something and it can help someone else, we are just helping each other out."

I was thinking, "No, you are just letting other people do the arduous work of getting all this stuff so they can grow in their lives for what they feel is part of their life path and their lives. Then you copy everything they are doing or getting. People work hard to be their own individual selves."

She would want to copy everything that I was doing on my spiritual journey, and then I came to realize that I was doing all this work to find all this information (I mean, years of demanding work—journaling; online classes; meditating; reading books; listening to podcasts; going to several lectures, which included Tony Robbins and Esther Hicks; two spiritual awakenings; several "dark knights of the soul" journeys; inner-child work; and the list just went on and on—and she was just riding on my coattails. I hated seeing this within myself. I was judging her, and I did not like it one bit. I thought that my spiritual journey had absolutely nothing to do with hers; my path in life was different from hers. And my destiny was completely different from hers.

I started thinking, "What is she learning for herself if she is copying other journeys?" For through my spiritual journey, the joy that I had found through these years of work had been inspirational, and I had grown tremendously. I was learning quickly that I had to be very selective in what I shared with her. I was seeing that if I told her things that were personal to me, she would tell everyone in my family before I got the chance to. A lot of times, I felt like I had to walk on eggshells with her and treat her with kid gloves every time I talked to her. I also felt several times that when we would try to have conversations over things that I was thinking about, she would get so mad and so defensive. It was like, "I am trying to have a conversation with you to understand you, and I really want you to understand me, and you are getting mad at me? I do not get it."

She would tell me that I was negative during some of our disagreements. Wait a minute, it hit me! Was I being negative in our conversations, or as I hitting the nail on the head? I struck a chord with her with the truth about herself, and she just simply wasn't ready to hear the truth.

And she would say that I brought negativity everywhere I went. And I was like, "Wait a minute, I am simply asking you questions on why you do the things you do, and you deflect the conversation and twist it all around to make yourself look good. And then you call me a name when I am trying to understand you, and then you say we can't have a normal conversation because we aren't on the same page? You are right, we cannot have a normal conversation because *you* have already made assumptions about me before we even started talking: I am this, and I am that, and I am negative. And *you* are having a conversation to respond to me or react to me, not to understand me or listen to me. So since you are only reacting to how you feel and only to what you are saying, you have no idea what is on my mind or what I am going to say, which means that we will not be on the same page because you are on your page and your page only!

"Then you commented to me on our disagreement that you cannot have a relationship with me because I do not meet your expectations. What? I do not meet your expectations?

Think about it: how will I know what your expectations are for me if we are not on the same page, as you said earlier, and you have not told me what they are? How long is this list of expectations that you have for me that I don't have a clue of?"

"Why would anyone in life have any expectations?" I thought. "How do I know what the next person is going to say to me or how they are going to feel? I have no idea; I am not a mind reader." But I was getting good at my intuition and how self-aware I was becoming. I was internalizing and seeing all these behaviors coming from her, and I was concluding that she was a narcissist and a bully. I saw that she wanted to be that alpha female in the pack, and I was starting to realize I did not want someone like this in my life.

Seeing all this within my sister, I knew that I had to go within myself to see and figure out why I was feeling this way about her, and these feelings that I was having were coming from within myself. I had to start working on my perspective toward her. A quote that had stuck with me came from one of my mentors, the great late Dr. Wayne W. Dyer: "Change the way you look at things, and the things you look at will change."

My husband and kids felt the same way I did about my sister. Every time he had a bonus coming in from work and he wanted to surprise me with something, my husband would get upset when my sister would call me and tell me when they were getting their bonuses. That would piss my husband off because he could never surprise me with anything because she would take away his thunder. Any time something exciting happened in my life, I would tell her first, and then she would tell the whole family before I got a chance to. It was frustrating. My boys could never understand why she would never invite them over to her house, which would piss me off because every time there was a holiday, I was invited, but my husband and boys were not. What type of family has this divide in it? So I never spent time with them on holidays. These were the things that I noticed constantly over the years, and I did not like it one bit.

8

New York

At this point in my life, I had been on a spiritual journey. I had tried to get my third ex-husband to come along for this beautiful journey, but sometimes he was on it, and sometimes he wasn't. I did not realize at this point that I was evolving and growing at an astronomical rate, and he was not. I have always worn my heart on my sleeve, and I want to believe the best in anyone.

We both got an opportunity to move to another state for a job that offered us a huge pay raise and much better benefits. So before we moved, my ex-husband and I decided to get married again. Second time to the same guy—who does this, right? My sister was living in that state, and she was working at the company that offered us a position. She said that we could move in with her until I sold my condominium and we found another place there. I had to wait for my youngest son to finish his senior year of high school because I did not want to move him in his last year; my parents moved when I was in senior high school, and it sucked.

So I put my condominium up for sale, and we started our jobs at that company. We stayed with my sister on the days that we worked, and we traveled two and a half hours back to our condominium on our days off. So we were at her house for three days one week and four days the next week; we worked twelve-hour days. We were on opposite shifts again until we could sell the condominium and my youngest son finished high school.

After ten months of doing this, my sister needed a knee replacement and someone to help her recover. I decided that it was too much traveling from state to state each week, my sister needed help, and my condo was not selling, so I quit that job so I could spend the rest of my youngest son's life as a senior at home with him. He had two months of high school left. So I stayed at my condominium with my son while my husband traveled back and forth. I took the condominium off the market for a couple of months until my son graduated.

While he was in school, he was getting into becoming a chef. They had culinary classes at his high school, and he was taking all of them. He met his girlfriend; her name was Emily. I loved Emily; she was like a daughter to me. She had a rough life growing up; she was in and out of foster homes because her mother was such a bitch and did not care for her. I always felt bad for her because she would try to do the right thing and have a relationship with her, but her mother was like mine, who just was not emotionally or mentally there or would always yell and scream at her. I always felt like we had a lot in common. We used to sit and have long conversations about her life, and when my son and she graduated from high school, he proposed to her, and they were planning to get married.

I had put the condominium up for sale again, and within two months, it was sold. I said to myself that it was all about timing. We ended up moving from Vermont to New York. Emily enrolled and got accepted to the Culinary Institute of America, which was two hours away from where we moved to. We were all so proud of her for getting accepted. While she was at school, my son got a job as a chef and was working and banking money for him and Emily.

After we moving to New York for only about three weeks, I went to the grocery store to pick up a few things that we needed at the house. I was driving down the road, doing forty-five miles per hour, when I had a green light at an intersection. I remember it was in October, and for fall, that day was nice; the sun was shining, and it was sixty-five degrees outside. I had my window rolled down in the car. Anyhow, I was driving through the green light in the intersection, and unexpectedly a van coming from the other side broadsided me, doing about fifty miles per hour. The next thing I knew, everything was in slow motion, I heard this big bang, and my airbags on the passenger side of my car went off. I had my seat belt on, but my airbag did not go off. The next thing I knew, my car skidded off the side of the road, and I did not know what happened until I looked over to the passenger side of the car; a total of six airbags went off, and then I realized that I was just in a car accident.

The first thing that I did was wiggle my feet and my legs, and I knew they were OK. Then I started moving my neck and arms, and they were OK too. The only thing that I was having problems with was breathing. I was breathing, but it hurt. People automatically came running over to my car to see if I was OK, and I told them, "Yes, it just hurts to breathe." And then the person from the other car came over and apologized profusely, and she told me that it was all her fault. I told her not to worry about it. She told me that she was on her phone, texting.

The police were called to the accident, and so was an ambulance. I was brought to the hospital, and I ended up with a fractured sternum and two broken ribs. I was so thankful that I was alive; it was going to take me months to heal, but I was alive and grateful. But my car was totaled; it only had twelve thousand miles on it.

To make a long story short, I got ahold of a lawyer and ended up having my hospital bills and my car paid off, and I got a huge settlement out of it. Three weeks after my car accident, I had to have my left knee replaced, not due to the accident but due to severe arthritis in it for years. I was out of commission for about six months in this new state. Welcome to New York!

Back to my son and Emily. He supported her all through school. When she had the time off, she would visit us and stay at our house. And she always used to come and bake all kinds of stuff for us to show us what she was learning in school. She brought us the most delicious cake and cheesecake that she made; I had never in my life had anything that tasted that good. I always had to remind her to shut our oven off because she never did after baking. I asked her why she always forgot to shut the oven off, and she would say, "We are taught at school not to shut them off. We always need them on so they are ready for us to use."

I used to call our house a bed-and-breakfast because it seemed like the kids would come home to eat, sleep, take a shower, and leave. I did not mind; I loved seeing them all. I was so proud of all our kids. My eldest son and his girlfriend had a baby girl, so my husband and I had three grandchildren at this point. Emily loved my granddaughter; they used to have so much fun together. And I loved spending time with my granddaughter; every time she visited, we would go on Snapchat and make Snaps. Aw, the memories I have with my kids and grandkids.

Emily was at our house in between classes. She was such a diligent worker. She would call me Mama. Any time my son would get mad at me for something, she would always yell at him and say, "Don't talk to your mother like that!" She was a good role model for him; she inspired him and helped him grow and mature. I admired the woman that she was with all the adversity that she had faced in her life. She inspired me to become a better mother and role model to my kids. I always felt like she was an old soul.

It was December 8, 2018, and it was any other normal day. Emily was supposed to visit us. We were texting and texting her because we did not know where she was; she was supposed to be there hours ago. So we were all worried about her.

After a while, my son and my husband went out looking for her. While they did, my son got a phone call from Emily's foster mom, and she told him that Emily had gotten into a head-on collision with a drunk driver, and she was killed instantly! She was only two weeks away from graduating from culinary school as a pastry chef. She was on her way to see us.

My son was twenty years old. This devastated our family, especially my son. He felt so guilty that he had asked her to visit us, and I told him that if she did not want to see him, she would not have come, so he could not blame himself.

He also said to me, crying hysterically, "Mom, how did you deal with this? How!"

And I told him, "Babe, this is going to be the hardest thing that you will have to endure in your lifetime. You will have to take each day second by second, then minute by minute, and then hour by hour, breath by breath. There is no given time on how long you will grieve because everyone is different. You must take it day by day. You will never forget, but time heals all wounds. The only lesson we can learn when we lose a life is how to live life."

I started to look at life from a different perspective. I started to look at the small things that we all take for granted, being grateful for all the blessings that we have (simple things such as running water, food, shelter, and electricity). You do not realize how much these things and the people you do have in your lives mean to you until they are gone. They simply can be taken away from us at any given moment like Emily. Life can change in the blink of an eye. Why do we get so mad at the simplest things? That is ego, being self-consumed when we do not get our way, like a five-year-old throwing a temper tantrum.

Why should anything bother us at all? Why does everyone take life so seriously? Life, to me, is just a big classroom where we are all in just learning; we are going to fail, and we will not learn anything if we pass every class.

I was asking myself why I was taking the hardest classes in life. I started to look at things differently, and I began to think differently. Emily's passing hit me hard and made me look at the whole theory of life. I came to realize that I didn't want to surround myself with people who are jealous of me, who want to compete with me, whom I must approach with kid gloves on, or whom I should walk on eggshells with the things that I want to say because I am afraid that I may hurt their feelings. (I felt this way my whole life; I didn't want to hurt people's feelings, or I didn't want confrontations.) I started to realize I am not responsible for other people's feelings but mine, period. Other people's feelings are within them, not mine, which they are bringing on themselves because of the way they perceive things; it has nothing to do with me. I did not want to be around people who dismissed me when I had something to say. I wanted to be around people who value and trust me and what I have to say. When people do not trust or value people, that, my friend, is insecurity that they have inside themselves. I chose to be around people who inspire and motivate me to want to do better in my life as I loved doing that with them as well. A collaboration at its best, I'd say. I chose to have these people in my life; if I could not have them, then I chose to go without. I was looking for quality, not quantity.

I have noticed since Emily's passing that I am becoming

even more aware of people's behaviors and actions and of my behaviors and emotions. I will quote a saying that one of my mentors has said: "The quality of our life is determined by the quality of our relationships that we keep, the quality of the relationships that we keep will be determined by the amount of trust that is in the relationship, and the amount of trust that is in a relationship will be determined whether two people can sense that the other is honoring and respecting them and taking them seriously!" That was said by Kain Ramsay. Thank you, Kain. That quote opened my eyes to a lot of the relationships that I have in my life, especially with my sister and my husband. I came to realize that I could not be around her because she did not inspire me, lift me, or motivate me to become a better person. I did not see her doing this with anyone in her life—my sister-in-law, her best friend, and my mother. I believe that I have overcome a lot of hurdles in my lifetime, and I respect myself enough to not want to be around people like this, people who do not see my value and that of others. I'm starting to see the value of the universe and our existence.

In February 2020 the world had come down with a pandemic—the COVID-19 virus. Millions of people had died during this pandemic; we had to socially distance ourselves, wear masks, wash our hands constantly, and get COVID-19 shots and boosters to stay alive. Scary times it was. I was fifty-six at this time. I never thought in a million years that

I would be in the middle of a global pandemic. The entire world had changed, people had to quarantine in their houses, kids could not go to school, businesses had shut down, and visitors were not allowed in hospitals.

My youngest son was twenty-two, and my eldest son and my husband's daughter were thirty years old. Our grandchildren were eleven, nine, and four. I could not imagine raising kids during a global pandemic. I would be scared shitless! It showed me how strong and resilient our kids were by doing this. My eldest son and his girlfriend and my husband's daughter and her kids caught the COVID-19 virus; they were all sick, but they all recovered and were doing well. I am so grateful that it was not worse.

On September 13, 2020, my mother passed away. She was one month away from her seventy-eighth birthday. She had a heart incident. She was living with her boyfriend with whom she had had an affair, and she was taking care of him as he was twenty years her senior. She just got to the point that it was just too much for her, and she did not have the energy to continue to do it.

My sister was devastated. When she called me and told me the news, I went to her house to comfort her. My younger brother came over as well. She was so distraught over her passing. I remember both of my sons wanted to come over to her house as well, and my sister was so distraught and said, "I'm just not up for any company. Right now is not the time."

My brother told her, "Well, I would like to see my nephews, so if it's too much for you, I will go over to the coffee shop and meet up with them." You could tell that my brother did not have that close of a relationship with my mother as well.

And I was thinking, "Who are you to say that they can't come over? She was my son's grandmother! If they want to pay their respects, they have every right to!"

My sister had a grim time getting over my mother's passing; she tried so hard to have a relationship with her. She was not married or did not have a partner, so she did things with my mother, and when she passed, that left a huge hole in my sister's life. So I noticed after my mother passed that my sister would call me every day and start to treat me like she did my mother. I decided that this was not a healthy relationship. I would love to have a loving relationship with my sister, but every time I tried to have a conversation with her, she got so defensive, abrasive, and angry. And I did not know how to change that in her. It was not my job to change that; she must do that on her own, and I could not take it personally.

Moving forward to 2022, I started to examine my life and the people who were in it. I had a dysfunctional relationship with my sister, and my husband and I started to see things from a different perspective. I was looking at things through a different lens and starting to see people for who they truly were.

I was over at my sister's house one summer day, and two

of my brothers were there as well. I had posted a picture of one of my brothers on social media, and my brother commented that he did not think it was a good picture of him. I loved the quirkiness of the picture, and I wrote that I was so happy to get to spend quality time with him since I had not seen him in years. My sister was making comments to my brother, saying, "I get why you're upset because I don't like pictures of me posted either."

And then she said in front of me and my brothers, "Why do you post all the time? And you need to take that picture down." That was the first post I had in months. I told her that I didn't post all the time and that I was not going to take that picture down because I liked it. And she picked up her phone, rolled her eyes, and was trying to prove me wrong about how much I post on social media in front of my brothers. When I saw her doing this, something exploded in my head. At that very moment, I disconnected from my sister, and my spiritual awakening started.

Why was it any of her business what I did and did not post on social media? Why did she feel the need to prove me wrong in front of my brothers and try to make me feel less than who I know I am? I saw for the first time who she was. I decided to walk away from her, and I had not talked to her since that moment.

My husband would watch the interactions between us, and he would say how pissed off he got by the way my sister treated me, but he was never there to back me up or stand up for me. I would fight with him over that. I would ask him, "Why are you not standing up for me? I would stand up for you if your brothers were treating you that way."

Then while I was trying to heal from that relationship, I started seeing my husband of twenty-nine years differently. I noticed that there was not any intimacy in our relationship for a while, and every time I tried to have a conversation with him about it, he would get mad and defensive. Every time I expressed my wants and needs, he would shut down and didn't care about how I felt. I would cry in front of him uncontrollably, and it did not faze him one bit.

It got to the point where he was blaming me because of his anger. I told him that he is responsible for how he reacts. I noticed his narcissistic behaviors, only thinking of himself and not making me a priority. He would gaslight me and blame me for how he felt. I would always tell him, "It has absolutely nothing to do with me. It comes from within oneself." Man, would he get pissed! He was so famous for stonewalling me. He would just sit there and not say a word to me; he would have no opinion or suggestions about anything. He looked like a little kid getting scolded by his mother. And I would tell him that he had no power in this relationship; he brought absolutely nothing to the table.

These behaviors got worse and worse and worse. I started to notice his change. He would spend hours in the bathroom three times a day on his day off, and I would always have to ask him if he was OK in there. I would say to him, "Who spends hours sitting on the toilet? Doesn't your ass hurt?"

He decided to see a therapist for his behaviors, and he constantly admitted that he had a problem talking and communicating with me; he would sit there and agree with everything that I would say. I would always tell him, "I would love to hear your opinion and perspective on things." His therapist had given him tools to use as well, and he had not used them. I told him that it boggled my mind why a person would go to therapy and not be open and receptive to the whole process. I began to see that every time we had a conversation, he was not open and receptive to me either.

What's the point of being in a relationship and trying to plan a future together when it is not two working on the process and only one does all the work? There was no equal give-and-take. What's the point of getting advice from a therapist and not using it to improve your life? You know your life is not working, and you admit that it's not working all the time, but you do absolutely nothing about it. That's insane to me. We also had not had sex in years, and that was a huge problem for me.

I was not putting two and two together, but out of the blue, the veil was lifted from in front of my eyes, and I was seeing things through a different lens. I saw that he was going to the therapist, and I was not seeing any changes. Then he went to his doctor to get some Viagra because he told me he had erectile dysfunction, but when he got the medication, he never used it. Man, was I pissed! I suggested several times to see a marriage counselor, but he kept making excuses. Then he told me that when he cheated on me twenty years ago, the guilt was getting the best of him because he never cheated on anyone in his life; he had always been cheated on, but he had never done it before. I always try to put myself in someone else's shoes, so I could understand that, but at that time, I did not know that I was being manipulated.

Living with a narcissist for so many years can change your life. They only think of themselves and no one else, they will blame you for how they feel, and they try to make you feel like you are wrong all the time. Your opinion simply does not matter at all.

I had been watching this for years and not really seeing it. Do you know what I'm saying? He kept pushing me away to the point where I would start sinking all the energy that I was putting into him into myself.

While all this was going on, I would spend a lot of time on my own and going within myself. I started to meditate every day and just be alone. It was like the world started slipping away from me, and I felt like I didn't belong in it anymore. I was asking myself, "Why would I tolerate the intolerable?" The pain that I was going through was excruciating. I was losing my family and my husband all at once.

9

My Spiritual Awakening

The year 2022 was when my spiritual awakening happened. I was seeing the people whom I was surrounded by on a much deeper level, and I realized that I had absolutely nothing in common with my family and my husband, and none of them inspired me or lifted me up as a woman. I would walk away from conversations with these relationships feeling so drained and depleted and depressed. I learned that I was in such a codependent relationship with these people that I had to get myself away from them; they were not serving my higher purpose in life. I was becoming much more aware of their actions by just standing back and observing.

I truly believe that breaking away from these people had a lot to do with divine intervention because when I would try to talk with my husband about anything, it was like we were two strangers, and we had absolutely nothing in common. This was a mindfuck for me because I would think,

"How can you know someone for twenty-nine years, which is half your life, and have absolutely nothing in common with them?" That was a very hard pill for me to swallow; it was like I was in an alternate universe.

It didn't matter how nice I was or what I said. He would get so angry and defensive at anything that I said. He kept saying, "I'm depressed."

I would ask him why. And he would say, "I don't know."

I would tell him, "Only you know what you want in life and why you're depressed. No one else does." The universe was showing me so much shit; it was like a movie.

I would wake up every day at 3:33 a.m. I always wondered why it was that time; little did I know that the universe was giving me messages or downloads. I also started seeing repeating numbers constantly every single day: 222, 333, 444, 555, 111, 11:11, 12:12. I remember drinking a cup of coffee, and I heard in my head, "Check his email." So I logged onto his computer to check his email, and he had memberships on several different dating sites. And I read all the messages that they were writing to each other.

Then I saw that he was writing a book when I started writing this one, and I started reading it. It was about the woman whom he had cheated on me with, and it was very sexual in nature. That was all I had and wanted to see.

When I brought it to his attention, of course, he lied about it. Narcissists do not know how to be accountable or tell the truth. I even showed him what I found, and he still denied it. "Please don't belittle my intelligence, you friggin' idiot!" After I showed him his emails, he logged out and changed his password, and I couldn't get back in.

Then that same day, I was on TikTok. My friend was a tarot card reader, and she was doing live readings for people. My sister was in the room, and my friend pulled a card for her. It said that she had walked away from someone or something, and my sister said that she did walk away from something, and it was the biggest blessing that had happened in her life. I knew that she was talking about me. My intuition is spot on, and the coincidences that are happening in my life are beautiful. I was thinking, "If she thinks that I am not a blessing, then I'm glad I'm not in her life."

I also thought, "Who thinks like that? Why would you want to think like that about anybody?" I don't want to be around anyone who feels that I am not a blessing in their life or who doesn't like me.

I would have a conversation on the phone with my twin brother, and he would tell me that my sister had to have surgery on her knee again. She alerted the hospital security to not allow me to visit her while she was in the hospital. I was thinking, "OK. Why would she think that? Why does she feel the need to alert hospital security? Does she think I'm going to hurt her, or am I a threat to her?" I hadn't spoken a word to her in six months.

So it got to the point that every time I had a conversation on the telephone with my brother, he would tell me comments that my sister was making about me, such as "She needs to learn how to treat people."

I was like, "OK." I raised three beautiful kids for thirty-two years, I took care of my mother after my father died for six years because no one else in the family wanted anything to do with her, and I took care of my sister through two knee surgeries, a gastric sleeve surgery, and seven eye doctor appointments. And I babysat her dogs three times so she and my brother and his wife could go on vacations. How dare she make that comment that I needed to learn how to treat people? And worked as a home health-care provider; I took care of the elderly.

The things that I was seeing and was very aware of were starting to blow my mind. I started to see the narcissistic behaviors and the gaslighting with her too. I cleaned my house and disconnected from my whole family and my husband of twenty-nine years. I learned that I am a very sensitive empath, and I take on others' energies. I was taking on all these energies, and I was feeling depleted. The way that they were behaving had absolutely nothing to do with me, and this was their journey that they had to work on. Deep down inside I felt that I did not want to be around people who were projecting onto me who they thought I was when

I knew I was not this person whom they were trying to make me out to be.

This was the very first time in my life that I realized profoundly that hurt people hurt people. Very powerful! I got to the point where I didn't want to talk to my twin brother on the phone anymore because I didn't want to hear what my sister had to say, but he would tell me anyhow. So I was seeing he was not respecting or valuing what I was saying. I saw that in my husband and my sister when I was talking to them also. I learned to set boundaries in my life for the first time. You realize when you set up boundaries in your life that people don't like it one bit. It's because they can't walk all over you like you used to let them do. Man, do they get pissed!

One of my boundaries was filing for divorce again from my husband. I couldn't take it anymore. When I filed for divorce, he was livid. He kept blaming me for threatening divorce all the time. I said, "Yup, why wouldn't I? You don't love me, you cheat on me, you blame me for everything, and you don't have any power in this relationship! I need a man who can stand in his power, protect me, make me a priority, have my back, and inspire me to be a better version of myself like I have done for you!" OMG, it was like setting the devil off when I said that.

After I filed for divorce, it got worse. I forgot to mention that the whole time that I lived in New York, I did not work because my husband said that he wanted to be the man of the house and to take care of me. He said that I worked hard my whole life and that I deserved to be retired, and he wanted me to stay home. It drove me nuts. I wanted to get a job, and he kept telling me I didn't need to. Little did I know that he was cheating on me the whole time, and he wanted me home so he knew where I was. I had a car with a three-year lease that ran out, and he did not get another car for me, so I was stuck in the house for two years. In those years he moved his girlfriend and their daughter from Vermont, where we used to live, to New York. (I found this out later.)

I finally hounded his ass and told him to get me a car, which he did. Once he got me a car, I got a job. I had to get out of there. I opened my checking account, took my name off the joint account, and started banking all my paychecks. Again he was so pissed. I kept telling him, "What the fuck do you expect from me? I can't live here with you anymore!" He found out that I had $10,000 saved, and when I went to work on a Thursday, which was only a six-hour shift, he had ransacked the house. When I came home from my shift, I thought that I was robbed. He took all his belongings. I was happy that he was gone, but I was also pissed because when he left, I had only one client to take care of, which was only six hours a week. I realized then that only a boy would do that and not a man. I realized also that that boy was so scared of me because he knew that I knew what was going on. After all, I was relentless with him. I emasculated him daily. I was so devastated because this boy had been my best friend for thirty years, and I never in a million years would expect this from him.

So when you think that this was finally over, it had just begun. After he left he stopped paying the mortgage and the lot rent, but he still paid the cable and lights, which didn't make sense to me. He didn't register my car and didn't tell me about it. I had to go to court and sit in front of a judge and pay her $120 so I wouldn't have my license suspended. I had to hire a lawyer, and I spent one year's pay to get half his retirement, from which I got him the job. And I walked away from a thirty-year relationship with not a dime in my pocket.

Then I put the house up for sale; he did nothing to help me sell it. I packed it up and sold it on my own. He was four months behind in the lot rent and mortgage, and they were coming after me. He didn't even want me to get half the proceeds from the sale when I was the one who put the down payment. In the seven years that I had lived there with him, I did not make one mortgage or lot rent payment. He did them all. But during our divorce proceedings, I was responsible for the four months' back payments. On top of this, when I left that house, I was homeless and did not have a place to stay because I used up all the money that I saved on fighting him with my lawyer. I was living in my car in November, wintertime! I had never in my life been so pissed and angry at anyone as I was with him. And I had never been treated like that by anyone. I did not know who my car lender was or the insurance company because he paid all the bills, I had to research to find all this out on my own because he was afraid to talk to me and emotionally unavailable; plus, he knew what the fuck he did, and he was scared of me. LOL.

Why would anyone be so malicious and vindictive toward any human being unless they are really—and I mean really—disappointed within themselves that they must take it out on someone else? I had been faithful, loyal, honest, and loving to this man; something was broken in him. I used to say to him, "*Who are you?* You did all this to me because you've been cheating on me with multiple women, and I have been faithful in trying to work on our marriage." That was fucked up on the highest level possible. I just couldn't wrap my head around this shit; say nothing about processing it. I just didn't have the capacity to think this way.

While this was happening, my boys were taking his side and not wanting to spend any time with me. So I hadn't been able to have a relationship with my boys. I don't know if it was because I filed for divorce from my son's father. I simply don't know.

I started to see a picture of him on social media with a new girlfriend, the woman he cheated on me with twenty-five years ago, and he was with his daughter, whom he gave up, and our son. I'm happy for him because he had a lot to make up for with her. Yeah, that boy threw me away like yesterday's trash, and it broke my heart. I think he had been with three different women since I left him. That was seven months ago, and I am still single and healing from this whole experience.

I have learned that when you think you know someone, you never truly do. I also know what a narcissist is and what gaslighting is, and I can see that I am being manipulated. I have worked extensively on myself and have learned that my ex always held it against me when I sold my condo and moved to New York. I told him that the condo was mine and mine only, and I had every right to do what I wanted with it. I also told him, "You're a grown man. You did not have to move to New York. You could have said no." He didn't, but he blamed me the whole time. Then it made sense that his payback for moving us to New York was cheating on me and doing what he did to me. God tells me that I have to forgive him, and I know I do because I can't keep hanging on to this anger, but I will never forget what he did.

The thing that hurts me the most is watching my boys take his side, not seeing the mask that this man wears and not caring what has happened to their mother. It just hurts, and I still work on this every single day.

A couple of months after my divorce from him was final and I sold the house, my twin brother passed away unexpectedly. My younger brother invited me up to the house at Christmastime because he wanted all of us to get together and pay our respects to my twin brother. My sister was going to be there. I told him that I did not want to go, but he insisted for my brother's sake. Now remember that at this point I had not talked to my sister in two years. I was very trepidatious on seeing her.

The minute I got up there, she was good. We had a good night, watched a movie, played some cards, and went to bed. On Christmas morning it was like the devil came out! She laid into me, telling me that my ex-husband had not slept with her friend from work and that she was very highly intuitive now. I didn't know what she was talking about. She also told me that my ex-husband was very happy with whom he was with and that he was better off without me. I was like, "Wait a minute! I haven't talked to you in two years because you read part of this book in the section about you, and you didn't like what I had to say. But now you're yelling at me because you think your friend from work didn't sleep with my ex-husband? Who the hell is this person?"

Then she dared to tell me that all I ever did was make it about me, and she was screaming at me when she said, "It's not all about you!" Well, number one, that shit scared me! I told her that what she didn't understand was that, in my whole life, it had never ever been about me, and now it was finally about me, period. Don't ever let anyone tell you who you are; you tell them who you are. And number two, I told her she needed to leave my room and get out of my face.

It blew my mind that I hadn't talked to her in two years because she was mad at me over this book, but the first thing she fought with me over was protecting her friend and my ex-husband. That whole situation just blew my mind.

My whole intention for writing this autobiography is to help others who have gone through the same or similar situations as I have with bully siblings, toxic relationships, divorces, and children who have passed away. I truly want to help and comfort people because I have done a lot of healing and have become a healer through this whole process. I have gained a lot of wisdom through all my experiences in my life. I sincerely love guiding and helping people see things from a different perspective.

My family is furious with me because I have written this autobiography, but this book is not about them. It is about my experiences in life and how I have healed and grown from them. And if they don't like it, I apologize. Like what my sister has told me, "It's not about you. Get over it!" And if you are mad about what I have written because it's all true and it's my story, then you are not as healed as you're portraying yourself to be, and you still need to do work on yourself. I am triggering something in you that needs to be healed. That is what I believe I am here for on this earth, to help people be more aware of who they are and how to connect with their higher selves. How well are you treating people? I am saying that from the deepest of love. Why would you not want to help someone who is going through what you have gone through, as traumatic as it was? If you're healed, why will you be mad if someone has written about it? You should be standing with pride and confidence that you have overcome these obstacles in life.

The whole purpose of life is to heal and inspire others to become aware of their limiting beliefs and become the best version of themselves. In my life I have gone through two spiritual awakenings and several dark nights of the souls. My life has brought me to my knees, screaming in agony. My awakenings have brought me to the deepest and darkest parts of my soul, and I have learned to transmute this energy into light.

God gets me up every day and guides me through life. I feel his presence, and I try to serve him the best way I know how. I have learned through God that I am a sensitive empath, an earth angel, a truth seeker, and a healer. I am here to shine the light on people's dark sides. People don't like me because I tell them the truth, and they are not ready to hear it. I have a very strong intuition, and I have learned how to discern people well.

10

My Healing Journey

My healing journey had been very difficult for me. I had been through so much in my life that it had traumatized me on so many different levels. I'd lost three children, my parents both passed, and I had been through four divorces, two of those were from the same man. I had to disconnect from my one and only sister because I felt she had no compassion for women and was a bully. My twin brother passed away as well.

I learned that my younger brother lied to me for years. We went out to lunch one day, and he told me that he had a confession to make. I said, "OK, what is it?" He continued to tell me that years ago when I was in a chat room talking to a psychic named Jessica, he told me that that was him.

I was like, "What!" At first, I didn't know whether to be mad at him or what.

I thought, "Who would do that to their sister? It is so sneaky and conniving!"

Then I thought about it some more, and I thanked him for telling me. I told him, "If it wasn't for you, I would not have started this spiritual journey, and those conversations that I did have with Jessica, or should I say my brother, in that chat room changed my whole trajectory in life." Reflecting on everything that has happened in my life had brought me to some very deep and dark places within myself. I had to analyze everything. Why was I choosing the people I was around, and why would I allow them to treat me the way that they did?

I can't believe my own family is doing the things to me that they did! What type of family does these things? I learned that I was abandoned and rejected my whole life. With all my husbands cheating on me and none of them being faithful, I had to look within myself and ask why they were cheating. I learned that since I was a child, my father beat me all the time, and I was learning at a very young age how to survive. I was very aware of my surroundings and the people around me. I also learned that I couldn't believe anything that anyone was telling me because their actions never matched what they were telling me. I learned not to read people's words, but I had to read their actions, energies, and vibes. It was very hard for me to get close to my husbands because I did not know if I could trust them. I had always had a problem with trust because of what happened to me. I had been cheated on, gaslit, backstabbed, lied to, manipulated and abandoned, and rejected repeatedly. Little did I know all these experiences had happened to me for a reason.

When I divorced my last husband, that threw me into the darkest spiritual awakening you could go through. I had never in my whole life been through so much pain. It was excruciating to the point where I was curled up in a ball in the back of a dark closet, just screaming hysterically, screaming for anyone to hear me, screaming to hear someone—anyone—say, "Everything is going to be all right, hun." I never once heard that from anyone.

You truly don't know the true definition of *pain* until you are by yourself with no one to be found and no one even remotely checking up on you to see how you are doing. Does suicide cross your mind? Abso-fuckin'-lutely! I wanted to commit suicide so many times. I was going to overdose on prescription drugs. I was thinking, "I'm here by myself. No one checks up on me. I'm in a gated community, so if I passed away, no one would know until I don't know when." I was so traumatized, so numb. I would cry hysterically from the minute I woke up in the morning to the minute I went to bed. So many dark thoughts went through my mind. My whole life was just coming up, and I was reliving everything that had happened to me all at the same time. It was like a movie playing repeatedly. Pain does not even describe what I was feeling.

I would wake up every day at 3:33 a.m. I would sit on the couch and drink a cup of coffee, and I would hear songs in my head. That was my one-on-one time with God. I would tell him exactly how I felt, and I wanted to know the truth about everything. I had been meditating for years, and it had helped me out a lot. I started getting downloads in my head. "You are an earth angel. You are a chosen one." I started hearing all kinds of things, such as "You are here to help people come to the light." I was also told that I had broken so many linear generational curses through my family's bloodline, and I ranked very high up in the spiritual world for breaking patterns of sexual and physical abuse with children, bullying, not being emotionally unavailable to people, and controlling my emotions and mind. I'm still working on some of these things; healing is an ongoing process every day.

God has taught me that I have no control over anything, and I have had to lay a lot of those burdens at his feet. I can't worry. I shouldn't have any expectations.

I learned that I had such a codependent relationship with my ex, and I loved him so deeply to the point where I was hurt. I was looking at him in the whole thirty years that we were together through God's eyes, through a higher perspective, when he was hiding behind a mask. There was no equal give-and-take in that relationship, and he was abandoning and rejecting me repeatedly.

Now when you ask God to show you the truth, get ready. You must make sure that you can handle the truth because, I tell you, the truth can hurt! What you see and what God sees are absolutely two different things.

The things that God was showing me about my whole family were blowing my mind. I couldn't believe what I was not seeing, but when he showed me, I was blown away. The best way I can explain it is that you are being transported into a different world because when God lifts the veil away from your eyes, you see things so differently; you truly see people for who they really are, not who you want them to be.

When God showed me who my ex was, I kept saying to him, "Who are you?" I couldn't believe the things that he was doing, and I swear to you, we could not be even near each other because there was like an invisible force field between us; that in itself blew me away. I felt God's presence protecting me. Once you see it, you can't unsee it. That was hard for me to get used to as well. When God shows you the truth, you must start a healing journey on that as well. You ask yourself the questions How could I have been so blind not to see that? Why did I put up with that for so long? God has told me that I had to go through the pain of that relationship to know my self-worth and to learn that lesson. I also had to learn that I can't keep taking care of people; it is time to take care of myself and learn to love myself again.

How do you learn to love yourself when you don't know what love is? I mean, I thought I knew what love was, but the love that I was giving was not being reciprocated. So if it's not being reciprocated, am I truly loving the right way? To be in my mind daily can trip me up because I overanalyze things to the maximum. I have learned to transmute energy, turning dark into light.

Pain pushes me forward usually. But I must admit that this divorce threw me back hard, stopped me in my tracks, and put me in deep depression for years. That was how hard and deeply I was in love with that boy; it caused me so much pain that I did not want to risk falling again for someone because I could not feel that pain again. I don't wish that pain on anyone. Like I said I am a very sensitive empath. I feel others' energy. I felt the pain that my ex was projecting onto me; he knew what he was doing, and I felt that he didn't care about what he did to me and what I was going through. He didn't look back; he didn't care that he was treating his only son's mother like shit and trash and the effects it could have on him, and he was doing it in front of him and getting him involved. I felt and took on all this energy. And it wasn't even mine to take on. The guilt, the shame—I could feel him feeling this within himself. I had to let all this energy go because I was feeling it. I knew it wasn't my energy because I had nothing to feel guilty about or ashamed of. I could never, in good conscience, do to another human being what he did to me.

What role model are you being for my son? What are you showing him as his father? Are you proud of the man you are so you can be a good, solid role model for him?

To be honest it scares me to watch all this because, as a mother, I can't teach my son how to be a man; that's his father's job. I sit back and watch this because I have no control; my boys have to learn and see who he really is, and I do believe the truth will always come out when they are ready to hear it.

11

Lessons Learned

These are the hard lessons that I have learned in life:

1. Do not ever spend time with people who underestimate your worth.
2. I want people to ask questions about me without jumping to conclusions or making assumptions about me. The only way you are going to know anything about me is to ask me. I am an open book. Do not be shy.
3. Get rid of all expectations in your life. When you do, you will never be disappointed ever again.
4. Remember, it is not what happens in our life; it is our perception of what has happened. That lesson has taken me years to learn, but I have finally got it.
5. We do not see things in life as they are; we see things in life as *we* are. Please go within yourself, my friends.

6. The only thing that is ever going to fulfill us in life is how much we have grown within ourselves and how much we help other people. We need to get out of ourselves and help others grow.
7. The whole purpose of having conversations with people is to gain insight and understanding. It's not about getting defensive and pissed off. When you get defensive and pissed off, that means you are not listening to the other person; you are just listening to your perception of what the other person is saying. So you are pissing *yourself* off.
8. The experiences that are happening in your life are a reflection of who you are as a person and your thoughts and beliefs.

These lessons that I have learned are priceless. At present I am sixty years old. I have two children who have grown into thriving, mature men, and I am so proud of everything that they do. My youngest son is a chef, and my eldest son is a maintenance facilities technician. I have two beautiful grandchildren, whom I love spending time with and spoiling as much as possible.

I have just gotten out of a challenging thirty-year relationship with a narcissist, and I think that if it were not challenging, how would I have ever grown or evolved into this beautiful, strong woman who stands here today? If I had known, I would not have learned. He has shown me what I want and what I do not want in life and a healthy relationship. Every time he pushed me away, he taught me that I do deserve to be loved, valued, and appreciated, and he taught me to love myself. He also showed me what unconditional love was. When someone does not make you a priority in their life, it has nothing to do with you; it is about them. You must realize that as long as you are loving no matter how someone treats you, that is the true meaning of unconditional love; and for that, I am eternally grateful and appreciative.

I am so proud of the woman I have become and the challenges that I have hurdled in my life. I have survived an abusive father, an emotionally and mentally detached mother, and siblings who are just bullies growing up and up to this day. I have had three of my children pass away (Billy, Justin, and Emily), and I have had four failed marriages, two with the same guy. I have survived a global pandemic in which millions of people have died. That in itself is fuckin' epic. And I have had eleven family members who have passed away.

I have always been drawn to draft a book and tell people about my life. I have concluded that after everything that I have been through, I love the person that I have become. I can only hope and pray that my two boys will read this book and get a better understanding of who their mother is and not just project their feelings about me through the lens of their perspective (or how they view me as a mother because of their life experiences).

I am grateful for my family for the many lessons that they have taught me. I truly know now that every behavior and action that I have seen in my life within other people through this lens has taught me every single time to go inside myself and learn who I truly am. It is not other people who make me mad or frustrated; I have learned that it is me who is frustrated with myself. That is enormously powerful. I enjoy every moment that I have on this earth, and I am looking forward to what is to come.

I can honestly say that I know now what Jessica was saying when she kept asking me repeatedly, "Do you believe in angels?"

I would always say yes, and she would say, "Good."

Love you all, and God bless.

About the Author

I am a single mother of two boys, and I am a private home health-care aide. I was born and raised in Vermont, where I lived until I was fifty-two. I moved and lived in New York for seven years, dreaming daily of moving South to a warmer climate. My children are all grown, and I have two beautiful grandchildren, whom I love to spoil as much as I can. I am currently single and divorced, twice from the same man. After my divorce was final, I moved out of New York and back to my hometown, Vermont.

I have always wanted to tell my story in hopes that someone can relate to what I have been through. I have a passion for helping people get through trauma, mental illness, depression, and abuse. I have always been an empath and have so much compassion for others, and I feel that, because of what I have been through in my life, I can relate to a lot of things.

I'm very excited to see what lies ahead for me. I love to change because I get bored easily. I truly love people and connections; I love learning about them and the experiences that they have had in life. I love to travel and spend time with my grandkids. I'm a simple and humble woman who genuinely loves people and places.

Right now I am living my life the best way I know how, and I am loving every minute of it—healing, growing, and evolving every single day. I have become a certified life coach; I am an earth angel and healer. Someday I dream of finding the right person to spend the rest of my life with, someone with whom I can cocreate a dream life with equal give-and-take. I'm in no hurry as I know who I want, and he must be just as healed as I am. The next person I will be in a relationship with must be the best role model for my boys. I want them to know and see what a good, healthy relationship looks like.

This girl has gained a ton of wisdom in her life. And if I can help anyone avoid the pain that I have gone through, that's what makes life worth it.

www.ingramcontent.com/pod-product-compliance
Lightning Source LLC
LaVergne TN
LVHW051950060526
838201LV00059B/3579